BEHIND THE BANANA CURTAIN

A wry look at Queensland in 37 uncommon stories filed from all over the state.

HUGH LUNN

untapped

ABOUT *UNTAPPED*

Most Australian books ever written have fallen out of print and become unavailable for purchase or loan from libraries. This includes important local and national histories, biographies and memoirs, beloved children's titles, and even winners of glittering literary prizes such as the Miles Franklin Literary Award.

Supported by funding from state and territory libraries, philanthropists and the Australian Research Council, *Untapped* is identifying Australia's culturally important lost books, digitising them, and promoting them to new generations of readers. As well as providing access to lost books and a new source of revenue for their writers, the *Untapped* collaboration is supporting new research into the economic value of authors' reversion rights and book promotion by libraries, and the relationship between library lending and digital book sales. The results will feed into public policy discussions about how we can better support Australian authors, readers and culture.

See untapped.org.au for more information, including a full list of project partners and rediscovered books.

Readers are reminded that these books are products of their time. Some may contain language or reflect views that might now be found offensive or inappropriate.

CONTENTS

HEADING NORTH

Each year, believe it or not, tens of thousands of Australians—mostly from Sydney and Melbourne—sell their houses, pack their Holdens, throw away their heavy suits and move to Queensland. It is a trend which is expected to increase in the same way as Americans in the 1920s and 1930s flocked to California seeking sunshine, beaches and the barbecue way of life.

With the elimination of state death and gift duties, Queensland has been attracting the retired and elderly as well as many young people searching for an alternative life style.

The comparison with sunny California is not so far-fetched. In the 1920s a steady drift started in America to California as the people in more miserable climates heard that those on the west coast were always out in the sun and wore shorts and threw away suits and ties and the houses didn't need heating. It came to be looked upon as a dream land and by the 1930s it was as though someone had turned the States on its side like a pan and everyone flowed towards California. If you believe the old story that everything that happens in the U.S. happens fifty years later in Australia, then that explains the steady shift north now.

California quite quickly overhauled all the other states and is now the most populous in the U.S. If the 'California Theory' is right then Queensland could become the biggest Australian state within half a lifetime.

Many people—both inside and outside Queensland—have asked me what it is that makes this expanding northern state so distinctive. And while everyone in Australia, it seems, has an opinion on Queensland, few have any idea at all what really goes on there. As the *Australian*'s feature writer in Queensland I soon realized this. A few years ago, for example, there was a crazy story from overseas that

Arab guerillas might be training on the Great Barrier Reef. I received the following instruction from Sydney: 'Hugh, we want you to ring up the Barrier Reef and find out what is going on.' How do you "ring up" a natural formation that is a couple of thousand kilometres long, most of it under water?

Another time I had to drive six hours west of Brisbane in the small staff Renault to write a story about the effects of the cattle slump on a grazier near Taroom. When an executive in the Melbourne office heard this trip was on, an instruction was passed to me that, while I was out there, I should continue on into the Northern Territory to the big Brunette Downs property which was also having difficulties with depressed cattle prices. Obviously no one in Melbourne realized that such a trip amounted to a fullscale expedition—even in the 1970s—requiring water tanks, emergency food supplies, extra fuel, and a four-wheel-drive vehicle. I'd probably have been gone for months. Eventually I drove back to Brisbane, caught a two-hour jet flight to Mount Isa and from there took a small plane to Tennant Creek in the Territory. Another small plane deposited me at Brunette Downs and, in the end, I found it was quicker to return through Darwin to Brisbane.

Such desolation and sheer distance are best illustrated by the story I've included in this collection, of the cattle drove I joined from Queensland into the Northern Territory, with a boss drover so tough he stubbed out cigarettes in the palm of his hand to avoid fires.

Distances in fact are so great in Queensland—and population so scattered—that when I interviewed George Mye on his Torres Strait island I was further from Brisbane than is Hobart. Once, when I had to get to Thursday Island, I found there was no plane from Cairns for three days. I rang the office and they wanted to know if there were any ferries. I had to patiently explain that although Cairns is "up near the top" it is still about a thousand kilometres from Thursday Island.

Then of course there was the time a cyclone was heading down the Queensland coast. I told my Sydney office it was due to hit Bundaberg in three hours and they suggested—ever mindful of my health and well being—that I drive there to write a blow-by-blow description of what it was like being in a cyclone. After I pointed out that Bundaberg was five hours away by car, and therefore I would not arrive until the cyclone had passed, the reply came: 'Oh if it's that far north get Charlie Wright to drive down from Townsville.' I broke the news to them that Townsville was more than a thousand kilometres further north, and so instead I flew into the cyclone—code name Daisy—and spent a terrifying night with her, an episode which is also recounted in this book.

Queensland is full of surprises, and the stories included here (many of which have been revised since first appearing in the *Australian*) show that Queensland *is* the different state—different in a number of important aspects. As I wrote in my account of *Joh: The Life and Political Adventures of Johannes Bjelke-Petersen* (UQP, 1978), Queensland has a much more recent tradition of frontier life. It's also an area subject to regular climatic violence in the form of cyclones, floods, fires and drought. Its orientation is far more rural and decentralized, and in reality closer to the standard Australian myth of the bush—a place where people still fight the elements for a living.

Queensland is also—as some of the stories here show—a place where people are more successful at fighting sharks than at fighting racial prejudice.

Not that it is easy to sum up the experiences of a couple of million people, many of whose forebears came all the way from northern Europe to live in a tropical climate where just thirteen minutes' exposure to the sun can burn white skin and where narrow noses can't cope with the humid air. Even in Brisbane, near the southern boundary of the state, the summer sun melts bitumen and footpaths become too hot to walk on with bare feet.

People from the cooler south don't appreciate these things. When Prime Minister Fraser took a party of journalists to Queensland's Torres Strait in 1977 his office issued us all with a list of necessities for this area of year-round heat and humidity. Sure enough, a useless "woollen jumper" was included, yet the most important thing—insect repellent—didn't get a mention. A mosquito net in fact is as necessary in Queensland as blankets are in the rest of Australia, and the "mozzies" are so desperate for blood in the tropics that they'll buzz up and down looking for a tear in the net or a tantalizing limb too close to the edge.

I grew up in Brisbane but it wasn't till I returned from seven years working abroad that I began to understand my home state. The following stories have been selected from almost a decade of reporting the sometimes weird but wonderful world of Queensland.

OUT IN THE SUN &
UNDER THE WEATHER

ALL THAT GLITTERS IS PROBABLY ON THE GOLD COAST

The problem with pretending to be a multi-millionaire just for the weekend is that one tends to find that one's friends and relatives are not really up to it. I first noticed this phenomenon when my tennis doubles partner (forehand court), Macca, arrived to visit me at what is possibly the biggest and most exclusive private residential block in Australia.

There are millionaires by the dozen in the monolithic 177-unit Golden Gate building which towers above Surfers Paradise on Queensland's Gold Coast. In this one building the golden people of Australia have together paid more than $15 million for their holiday units. And it was here that I was booked in to the $350,000 penthouse above them all to see what it was like to be a multi-millionaire ... for one precious weekend.

Macca—with the choice of two acres of underground car parking—parked his rusting 1964 Valiant between a Rolls and a Jag. It wasn't so much the old car—they could have mistaken him for a rich eccentric—but rather the inverted wire coathanger for an aerial which stamped him, unmistakeably, as working class.

Then, in front of several millionaire guests at my lavish cocktail party, he looked at the view along forty kilometres of surf beaches, at the big mango moon above the curved ocean horizon, and at the lights of Surfers Paradise and exclaimed 'Wow', and then 'Good grief', and finally 'Crikey'.

I suspect he even made the porter feel superior. On the journey to the thirty-third floor the porter passed the time by listing the number of millionaires and describing the sort of people who own units. 'We have three psychiatrists, a famous heart surgeon, a professor of surgery, twenty-two doctors, twelve lawyers, six Jumbo pilots ...' he said.

'We don't mind, as long as they don't bother us,' replied Macca.

Then, after lazing around my rooftop pool for several hours he complained to the maid that he was surprised more people in such a big building didn't use the pool. She had to break the news to him that this pool belonged exclusively to the residents of the penthouse.

One can explain away one's friends—it is more difficult with one's family. My brother Jack arrived down from Brisbane and, in front of the servants, handed over a brown paper bag. 'We picked you up a pie on the way down,' he said. And mum and dad. They had never seen, nor imagined, such luxury ... three bedrooms, several balconies, a powder room, my own sauna, a green lawn (artificial) beside the pool, a barbeque.

Mum, a proud Gold Coast girl born and bred, looked down at the sights and said: 'This is where your uncle cut his leg with a broad axe while splitting logs.'

Despite it all, I adjusted to the good life myself without difficulty, although I must admit there were a couple of awkward moments. When I arrived the housekeeper, Brownie, asked what I would like for breakfast the next morning.

'Two Weetbix, no sugar,' I said.

'Oh Mr Lunn,' she said, shaking her head with disappointment, 'you'll never be a millionaire if you talk like that.'

My champagne cocktail party was going well until I asked the retired admiral if he had travelled on his recent world tour by plane or boat. 'My dear fellow, I think you mean a ship,' he said amid much laughter. But then the admiral kept confusing people by asking them what "deck" they lived on in the building.

Because I was in town the mayor, Sir Bruce Small, naturally arrived for a courtesy visit. 'Are you looking for capital gain or a return?' he asked. I wasn't sure. 'No, no, no, Hugh. A millionaire will always reply "That is an unnecessary question",' said Sir Bruce. 'He knows that if he earns a million dollars in interest he will pay $666,000 in tax. But even if he only makes $300,000 in capital gain, because he pays no tax, he makes more than if he got a return of a million dollars.'

In the group was an Australian multi-millionaire who was "in timber". He was talking of the problems of being a millionaire. 'When I had only eleven employees I ran everything and I got all the bottles of scotch and legs of lamb. Now with over a thousand employees it all goes further down the line. My employees really own the company. They run it. They see it.' He then reached into his pocket and slipped me a case with a fourteen carat gold pen in it: 'Here, take this and make sure you write nice things about millionaires. It isn't as easy as people think.'

I stumbled to another group and again gave my origins away. A millionaire was talking. He had a wallet full of "black" money, he said, but the stuff he was handling looked colourful enough.

'Black money?' I said, and everyone in the group went quiet.

'You have just given yourself away,' he said. 'Everyone in the millionaire class knows what black money is. It is money on which tax hasn't been paid and it can't be banked or invested and must be spent. It is usually found in wallets.'

By the end of the cocktail party I decided I would never make it, not in one weekend. So I got myself a tutor. A couple of floors down was just my sort of millionaire—Lance Summergreen, an egalitarian millionaire in his mid-thirties who'd made his money shifting dirt in trucks.

I rented an extra unit to get rid of Macca and Lance stepped into the breach. He is moving the dirt dug out for the Melbourne Underground—and it isn't easy to find places to put it. The further Lance has to cart the dirt in his trucks the more it costs him, so he hires helicopters and flies around Melbourne looking for holes in the ground that he can fill. 'The trouble is people are waking up that a hole in the ground is worth a lot of money,' he said.

As we talked about such unusual investments the telephone rang and I rose. Lance, a man with the build of a truck driver, pushed me back in my seat. 'Let the housekeeper come up and get it,' he said. It was Ray White Real Estate asking if I could mention that they were the managing agents for the Golden Gate apartments. I said I would see if it fitted into the story.

'You are hopeless,' said Lance. 'You don't even think like a millionaire. You should have said "What's in it for me?"—that's how millionaires get to own these penthouses.'

Over lunch Lance pointed out the Royal Doulton china we were eating from. 'Don't ask the difference from normal china—it is like asking the difference between clay and chalk,' he said.

He explained that he and the other millionaires had bought Golden Gate apartments because, while there are hundreds of different unit blocks available on the Gold Coast, the biggest and best will always attract the clientele with money. It provides an investment that can be rented for $400-$500 a week in season and—because the rich owners can take long holidays whenever they want—it becomes a free apartment for themselves out of season.

'For example, even though $350,000 sounds a lot this penthouse would be a good buy.'

I agreed it was a great spot to stay—I especially liked the five-metre-high bedroom ceiling with the glass wall overlooking the Gold Coast below and the stars above.

'Aren't you forgetting again,' he said. 'I am talking about buying it to make money. They'll never build it cheaper again.'

Maybe not, but perhaps there are other reasons for buying into what one woman resident almost nostalgically called "this last bastion of capitalism".

Few people know as much about the building as Louise Foster who lives on the eighteenth floor and works on the seventeenth. Louise went into real estate almost twenty years ago after she met a top Gold Coast real estate man in a local fruit shop while buying a pound of bananas. 'He offered me a job after we talked for a while and I sold a block of land and got £750 commission and a £500 bonus and I thought "What have I been doing all my life that I haven't been in real estate".'

Louise retired a few years ago, and when the Golden Gate was opened in 1977 she bought a unit. The management asked if she would mind selling some.

'The buyers are not all doctors and lawyers. There are about four car dealers and see that fellow over there, he used to drive a bulldozer and he paid $95,000 cash. There are two publicans from north Queensland and a service station owner from out west. I bought here myself because there is a view while you do the ironing and the people who live here are the type who have travelled and are interesting to talk to.

'Take one millionaire I sold a suite to. I showed him one of the six units on a certain floor and he said "I'll take it." I asked if he didn't want to look at the other five. "Are they any better than this?" he asked. The sale only took a few minutes and then he asked me what was my favourite perfume. "Promise her anything but give her Arpege" I said, and he reached into his briefcase and pulled out a bottle of Arpege.'

Len McNeil, a Qantas Jumbo captain who bought three units for a quarter of a million dollars, thinks the Golden Gate is the best thing he has seen on his world-wide travels.

'You have been to the States I take it?' he asked me—No.

'You would have been to Honolulu?'—No.

'Oh well you would have seen *Hawaii Five-O* on TV—well the building I am talking about comes on right at the start of that.' Now he had reached my level.

Len, who retired recently, said that he had stayed in the best accommodation around the world for Qantas. 'When I went looking for units I made up a check list like we have on a Jumbo where you don't proceed to the next item until you have a favourable response from the previous item.' His first question for the salesmen was 'Where did you get the sand for the concrete from?'

The reason for this was that he had stayed in a luxury hotel in the Middle East where beach sand was used and the salt in it corroded the iron reinforcing. "They were hammering day and night repairing it and I couldn't get any sleep," he said.

Satisfied that they used water-washed sand for the Golden Gate he tried some masonry drills on the walls and bent three. Then came the all-important question: what sort of garbage system?

'Garbage disposal in seaside units must be good because people eat seafood which can stink the place out very quickly,' he said.

He liked the fact that it was a bit back from the beach. 'I own units at Forster on the New South Wales coast and when you are right on the beach people walk sand into the building and sand and carpets don't mix. I could see from the units that the people who would live here would be on my own plane and wealth, and would be people I could talk to. And I have found the class of people in the Golden Gate to be better than the people you meet at the Ilikai in Honolulu.'

Originally, he said, he only intended to buy one because he had units in Sydney, but he liked it so much he bought another. 'Then something was still gnawing at the back of my brain and I thought "That's what it is. We will get another bastard".'

But Len doesn't think Jumbo pilots are paid too much: 'No one pays you a lot of money unless you earn it. Jumbos cost $80 a minute to operate. You would have to be Solomon to say what is a correct salary but the thing that impressed me was that I once worked out that the eighteen top Qantas pilots were paying a combined tax of $3 million a year. I used to sit up there in the ironmongery in thunderstorms at 2 a.m. with every nerve in my body screaming for rest and think to myself "If I am getting 34 cents in the dollar who is winning at this game?".' That is why he started investing in real estate for capital gain years ago. 'I couldn't extol the virtues of real estate enough,' he said.

And Len means it. On one of his flights from Honolulu to Sydney he said he hit the Australian coast right over the Golden Gate. 'I did a bit of a bank and gave the passengers a bit of a burst on the Golden Gate.'

Not all the investors are men nor do they all live in Australia. Miss Elaine Bermingham owns a couple of units but although she's a native Australian she has lived in California for the last twelve years. I gave her a call from the penthouse. 'Hang the expense,' said Lance, 'charge it to the Golden Gate.'

Miss Bermingham said she had opened the Kay Rent-a-Car offices in Brisbane and the Gold Coast years ago but could see that she would never get anywhere in Australia because she was a woman. 'I'm no woman's libber or anything like that,' she said, 'but I couldn't get a bank loan in Australia and I had to go to the U.S. to start my own business. But I'm still an Australian and in the last eleven years I have been home seventeen times.'

She set up the "Australian Kangaroo Club" with its headquarters at Newport Beach near Los Angeles. 'It was my brainchild and it now has 10,000 members throughout the U.S. and Australia. I concentrated on family reunions and improved relationships between Americans and Australia. I was a stranger in this country and it was very difficult and I could see there was a need to help Australians and Americans get together.'

She said she had invested in single family residences in California which in the last five years had shown a 400 per cent return but that had now levelled out. 'I had no idea anyone in Australia had the capability to attempt something of the size of the Golden Gate and I think it has as much potential as any of our investments here in California.'

Are you a millionaire Miss Bermingham? 'Let's say I don't sit down and work it out. But it will come if I am not already.'

The Golden Gate has certainly added a new vertical dimension to garish Surfers Paradise. At the top of the building—hundreds of feet above the thongs—there's a millionaire scrap metal dealer, a wholesale fruiterer, and an admiral, and apparently a submarine commander was negotiating for a unit near the bottom.

But I found the trouble with my temporary status was that people didn't fully appreciate it. I walked down Cavill Avenue in Surfers and it was obvious no one realized I was staying in a luxury penthouse. I did try this piece of information out on a waitress who replied: 'Isn't that funny, so do I. I thought I'd seen you somewhere before.'

Maybe it didn't help that I began the conversation by saying 'I work for ...' and Lance broke in saying 'No you don't work for anyone. They work for you.' No wonder the rich have traditionally gambled—not to win, but that others might see their wealth: to show it doesn't matter if they lose.

Lance eventually gave up on me. 'I can't see you ever buying this apartment,' he said, adding in exasperation, 'Just what is your personal ambition?'

I want to improve my backhand, Lance.

JUST A BIG PILE OF MEAT

Paul Howard must have been a sight as his tall frame emerged from the surf bathed in blood after such a diabolical fight with a shark that at one stage he thrust his arm down the shark's throat. He got into the fight at Kingscliff beach to save a girl on an air mattress, and ended up with eighty stitches worth of wounds.

But instead of seeking help he pulled two little girls out of the water, yelled to warn some board riders and then moved along the beach to tell a man and his daughter to get out of the water. He got the local garage man to run along the beach warning others and then told the local lifesaver to close the beach. A man and his wife stopped him as he walked—covered in blood—a couple of hundred metres to his car, but he refused help telling them he was all right.

The lifesaver wanted to take Howard to hospital saying 'It's our job' but Howard told him: 'I prefer you to close the beach.'

He set off in his car for the hospital—chased by an ambulance with its siren going. He stopped, let an ambulance man bandage him, but wouldn't let the ambulance take him to hospital and drove off towards the Tweed Hospital eleven kilometres away on his own. But all the while he was losing blood and he apparently blacked out and rolled his car.

'I wasn't feeling badly on the beach,' said this laconic Queenslander, 'and anyway I knew where the hospital was.'

How? 'Well I had driven there before, once for nine stitches in my head and another time when I hit the rocks at Schnapper during a cyclone and I got seventy stitches in my leg plus they took a bit of bone.'

Why wouldn't he go with the ambulance? 'I was driving along making good time, but bleeding a lot, when I heard a siren. I didn't take much notice of it. It kept going and I could see them way behind me but I still kept driving. After about three kilometres I thought suddenly that they might be after me so I slowed down in case they were. There was only one of them and he stopped me. He mopped up blood and bandaged me and asked if I was all right. I said "I'm OK" and he said the cuts were pretty deep and I said "Yeah but I'm still all right." I'm a glazier and I get cut all the time. The ambulance had another emergency and I didn't know how many of them there were and I kept thinking about the $60 they would charge. So I said I could make it all right. But with a few kilometres to go—it's a bit hazy—but I sort of felt weaker and weaker and eventually blacked out and rolled the car. The ambulance came and gave me a whole heap of painkillers and I had to pay the $60 anyway.'

Before the day was over Paul Howard was on his way back home with his parents to Brisbane after signing himself out of hospital despite his deep wounds. 'They cracked right up but, I don't know, I just don't like hospitals.'

As he sat in the lounge chair at his Brisbane home drinking lemonade I could see how close he had been to that shark. As well as the bites which were covered with bandages and still bleeding, there were long scratches on his chest, shoulder and hands from contact with the shark's rough body.

He told me how it happened. He'd been surfing at another beach that day, and decided to leave—not because of a shark which cruised in near him, but because the water was too crowded with other board riders. He is after all used to danger—in his job as a glazier he puts in glass windows on high rise buildings, or swings from cables re-sealing and cleaning them.

Kingscliff—just over the border—looked quieter so he started surfing there.

'I noticed a girl paddling around on a blow-up mattress. About ten minutes later I saw a fin in the water but I didn't worry, I just thought it was a porpoise. We often surf in schools of porpoises. At this stage I was about fifty yards out from the girl and I took off on a wave and came to within about ten feet of her and pulled out of the wave and I was just gonna go back out. I remembered the fin and I realized it hadn't come up at all as porpoises do and I thought "Shit, it's a shark."

'I saw the shark go under her. It did a couple of circles around her, then started charging in from a distance. There were two little sharks swimming around with it. We were only about fifteen yards from shore near the edge of a gutter and she was splashing a lot and I looked around and saw the fin going straight for her. I was laying on the board and on a wave and I speared in and pushed her well and truly forward and as I did I told her to get out of the water. She probably thought I was abusing her. At the same time as I pushed and yelled the shark twisted its whole body sideways and bit the back piece out of the board. It was just my reflexes I think but I sort of twisted at the same time it did—if I hadn't I would have lost my leg.'

Then began an amazing battle, which could be described in terms of "Man Mauls Shark".

'I don't think the shark was really that interested in me until I chimed in. Chicks on surf mats don't use flippers and they do a lot of splashing—plus there were other kids in the water doing a lot of splashing, whereas we don't get attacked much because we use rhythmic movements of our arms for getting around and we don't have to kick to catch a wave.

'Next it hit the front and I rammed its body with the point of the board and it started biting on the board. I went for its eyes because they reckon it's about the best place to hit a shark, that or the nose.'

Using all the power of his six-foot-four footballer physique, Howard lunged at the eyes. 'That's when I pushed my arm down its mouth—you can see the drag mark right down my arm muscle, it's pretty deep, and the rip across my hand. Its body was rough like sandpaper and when it bumped into me it gave me these cuts down my chest. That was just about it. Waves were coming in all the time, which was lucky, and pushing us closer to shore. My hands were all nicked and sliced from grappling with the shark and pushing it away'—he even had stitches in the ends of his fingers.

But did he manage to hit the shark?

'Oh yeah. After he bit my left leg and had taken another piece out of the surfboard I landed a good one with my whole fist right in his eye. It was with my good hand, but I don't know how much I hurt the shark, it was too busy thrashing around. I couldn't even tell how big it was ... except it was bigger than me. They are just so strong you wouldn't believe it. It would take a lot more than a hit in the eye to hurt them. Really I just didn't know where I was hitting it—but yeah, I got him in the eye once for sure. I hit him several times while keeping my board between him and me as much as I could—though he bit the point off. He bit the board in four places and I think it was the taste of fibreglass that scared him off rather than the several punches I landed.

'It was the surfboard that helped me—he would have bitten off my leg in the first place if I hadn't had the board. You see the board was seven foot long and no part of me was hanging over the edge so I fought him from the board although I nearly came off a few times and rolled around it a bit. Even with the pieces bitten out of it my board was still floating,' he said.

Howard has played first grade professional rugby but gave it away to surf—which he does each weekend from dawn until dark with a break at 8 a.m.

Later in the garage his mother showed me the surfboard: the pointed front was bitten off, a plate-sized chunk, still bloody, had been bitten out of the side with a tooth still embedded, there was another bite in the tail end and one underneath.

'Paul is the most casual person you will ever meet,' his mother said. 'He is too casual for his own safety. He plays everything down.'

But Howard did admit that he got close enough to find out what the shark's skin felt like, and he said the smell from his board shorts was enough to make his mother sick when she washed them—'because of the garbage from around the shark's mouth and the parasites that got in them'.

Because Paul Howard board rides each weekend—rain or winter—he has seen plenty of sharks. 'We see heaps. They usually don't bother you. This one wouldn't have gone for me, though I have seen a couple make a run at us. I had one chase me down the face of a wave once and I turned and he turned and that was it. They don't worry me because it is their territory, I am the intruder, they have been there a longer time than us.'

Howard said he loved surfing because he was constantly matching himself against the sea. He trains with weights twice a week to keep fit for surfing. His other hobbies are hang gliding and trail bike riding. What he loves most of all though is surfing with porpoises. 'I have been in with a school of four to five hundred. They love to play and a couple will get either side and a few beneath the board and when I turn they turn and when I pull back over the wave so do they. You have a ball but I worry sometimes I might hit them as I don't want to hurt them. They are so beautiful. Sometimes even though there is a great surf running I sit and watch them go through the waves. They are magic through the water. They turn so perfectly and are so artistic in the water.'

Paul Howard is tall and handsome with light blue eyes and white teeth, but he says his sister reckons he has had so many stitches he looks like Frankenstein 'except I haven't got two bolts in my head'.

Howard had the stitches out and was planning to be back on his surfboard down the coast less than a fortnight after the attack. He said his injuries healed well 'because I eat heaps of the right food'. He has had his nose broken four times playing football and had broken almost all his fingers at some stage. 'That's only natural,' this Queenslander said.

'My sister reckons that if they took all the stitches out of me I would be a big pile of meat on the floor.'

WAY BEYOND THE CALL OF DUTY

Go visit the Barrier Reef—all expenses paid, they said. What they didn't say was that Australia's Great Barrier Reef has two faces. One image is of blue lagoons and coloured coral in calm waters. But the reality—far from the tourist islands comfortably close to the mainland—is desolation and isolation: a stark panorama of imagined and imminent dangers. I found this while in search of a frail platform built in an angry sea on the edge of the inappropriately named Pacific Ocean. This is civilization's smallest, and possibly its most tenuous, outpost: twelve feet by eight, situated three hundred kilometres northeast of Cairns, and held to the earth by eight wires, some tied around coral.

Perhaps I should have realized what surprises lay in store as my path followed the trail of Captain James Cook who found the Outer Barrier so dangerous that he was concerned he might be charged with "timorousness and want of perseverance". More than two hundred years later nothing much has changed out there on the real Barrier Reef Australians never see, and I too worried about charges of timidity when my better judgment told me not to spend the night on that tiny platform.

To reach the platform I flew more than sixteen hundred kilometres north from Brisbane to Cairns then on to Cooktown (where Cook repaired his *Endeavour*) and another hundred kilometres out to sea to Lizard Island where there is a scientific research station.

The twenty or thirty scientists from all over Australia who spend a lot of time there studying the surrounding reefs lead a monastic life under canvas. A young Ph.D student from Sydney, Greg Stroud, emerged from the water in his black wetsuit just after sundown outside my tent with its hand-made wooden furniture—the driftwood suite. Only his long beard proved he was human. Greg had been sitting underwater for eight hours as he does every day studying the lives of fish (scientists call them "fishes" because of the differences in species). Since 1976, Greg has spent some three thousand hours sitting on the bottom, some of it after dark, learning where and how the fish sleep.

The director of the station, Dr Barry Goldman, mid-thirties, ex-Sydney, has been working on reefs for more than a decade and—like the other scientists—he has become much more attuned to the fish world. He walks past with a big torch in one hand, says hello, and plunges into the water as if it isn't there to swim out and check the boats before going to bed.

Dr Goldman is one of the men responsible for building the platform. The weather is too rough to go, he tells me. In fact the platform is in such a dodgy position that a week passes and it is still cut off. Dr Goldman tells me about the reef and why scientists must sit on the bottom. He alternates between the Aussie and the scientific idiom: 'When it is all said and done we know bugger all about it.' He and others built the platform because all of the research has been done in the reef areas close to the mainland and population centres and not out on the actual Barrier Reef. 'It's another world altogether out there,' he says. 'That's the thing that is sixteen hundred kilometres long and only a few fishermen and divers ever see.'

Lizard Island is dominated by a 370-metre mountain which was what attracted Captain Cook to the spot 208 years ago. He climbed the hill to see what he was up against in the Barrier Reef before heading out, past where the platform is now located, to escape. So I followed his footsteps to the top, an exhausting journey which left me with admiration for Cook's fitness.

From the summit, the actual Barrier Reef was clearly visible out to sea stretching like a ribbon of Gold Coast surf as far as the eye could see north and south, the waves of the Pacific pounding against an undersea barrier of coral probably two hundred metres high. Cook though did not enjoy this striking view at all: 'To my mortification, I discovered a reef or rocks laying about two or three leagues [ten or fifteen kilometres] without the island extending in a line NW and SE farther than I could see on which the sea broke very high.'

But as I looked for the platform (had I known how small it is, I wouldn't have bothered) I noticed a feature that also gave Cook some heart—narrow breaks like river entrances between some reefs. It was through one of these, just to the north of the platform, that Cook escaped.

There is something strange about Lizard Island—perhaps it is the isolation, or the history—and I soon discovered how eerie it was being lost on that mountain. When I reached the bottom it was already dark and, unlike Cook, I didn't have a boat so I set out to cross the island on foot to get back to camp. It was raining and in the island bush I inevitably became lost. I tried to move around via the beach but the incoming tide forced me up on to the rocks and in the pitch dark I made my way ever faster up and down and across, stumbling and falling, while the director searched for me.

I came upon a small crumbling stone wall—and recognized it as the remains of the home of another person who found that Lizard Island was not a nice place to be left alone. A century ago—in 1881—Mrs Mary Watson's husband went away fishing and while he was gone a party of Aborigines arrived in the night and killed one of her two Chinese servants. Mrs Watson fired a rifle and revolver at the Aborigines and they disappeared only to return the next day when they speared the other Chinese servant, Ah Sam, seven times. However, he managed to get back to the stone hut.

On the fourth day, Mrs Watson decided she had to escape with her seven-month-old baby, Ferrier, and the wounded Ah Sam but she had no boat. Desperate, she put them both in a small, square iron tank and paddled out to sea.

She kept a diary which told of her week in the tub, ending on October 11 with this final entry: 'Ferrier more cheerful. Have not seen any boat of any description. No water. Near dead with thirst.' The monsoonal rains started a few days later and when she was found in January, the tank was half full of fresh water. Her right hand still clung to a loaded and cocked revolver. Mrs Watson's monument in Cooktown reads:

Five fearful days beneath the scorching glare
Her babe she nursed
God knows the pangs that woman had to bear
Whose last sad entry showed a mother's care.

I was cut and bruised and caked with sweat when I emerged on the sandy beach outside the scientific station. My thigh muscles were like jelly and no longer working; my hands, feet and shins lacerated. And still the platform was to come.

Despite the weather, Dr Goldman agreed we couldn't wait for ever. He and I and research assistant, Hugh Sweatman, were going. Hugh spent all morning putting the gear into watertight containers.

Our boat battled waves bigger than itself all the way out. It took more than an hour and every time we bounced on another wave a bucketful of seawater hit me in the face.

The platform appeared in the middle of the ocean looking like a tent frame with no canvas. On closer inspection it was made out of steel scaffolding pipes painted white. Each of the nine pipes had a heavy piece of concrete cemented around the bottom to hold it down. There were three horizontal levels of steel bars: one which goes under in high tide, another for the living area, and a third to hold the roof. From each corner pole two steel guy-wires stretched like tent stays out into the coral bed where they were tied around coral or cemented into crevices. Each side was braced with a diagonal steel bar and a permanent ladder ran up one side.

The platform itself was twelve feet square but the living area only twelve by eight to leave some roof overhanging because of the heavy tropical rain. There were no railings on the living area, but on two sides a couple of boards could be roped into position to ward off the wind. If you rolled or walked in your sleep you joined the fish.

The first difficulty was getting from the boat to the platform. Barry and Hugh both climbed over the windshield of the boat, stood on the bucking front, and at the right moment nimbly jumped off onto the scaffolding. Then it was my turn. Hugh tried to hold me as I attempted to ease myself from the boat to the platform, but the rise and fall of the ocean is stronger than an arm and I all but landed in the drink. The only solution was to leap and grab.

Barry—in his long-armed, long-legged black wetsuit—was so much part of nature that he rode the front of the boat with a plastic crate in both hands and leapt into the structure. With his curly dark hair he looked like some trained animal climbing around the structure, up over the roof and down to the boat again.

The platform floor was covered in sea bird droppings and, so that we could sleep more soundly, Hugh and I scraped it off with a trowel and then scrubbed the deck with sea water. The platform was built especially for Hugh's underwater observations in the surrounding waters and his biggest gripe was the bird dung, especially when it washed down off the roof. Barry was up there filling holes to prevent this.

Three hundred metres further out the big waves kicked up by the Trades rose and crashed against the barrier which no one really understands and which we were here to find out more about.

I couldn't see land in any direction. Everything was sea mist, white-capped waves and the roar of wind and surf.

Captain Cook was within a few kilometres of here when he wrote: 'All the dangers we had escaped were little in comparison of being thrown upon this reef where the ship must be dashed to pieces in a moment. A reef such as is here spoke of is scarcely known in Europe, it is a wall of coral rock rising almost perpendicular out of the unfathomable ocean, the large waves of the vast ocean meeting with so sudden a resistance make a most terrible surf breaking mountains high ...'

Not far from the platform, waves foamed and rushed as they hit coral outcrops rising straight from the bottom. It was these columns that Hugh was studying. Studies on small artificial reefs close to shore appeared to show that the predatory character of many reef fishes kept numbers down and limited competition. It is thought that this may be why there are so many fish varieties on the reef. Hugh had to test the theory on these big isolated outcrops in real reef conditions. He had made wire grids around each outcrop and sat under the water watching and counting eight different species of fish. Although there are hundreds of types, eight was as many as he could do.

The wind was so strong that a bucket blew off before I could catch it—but it had been tied on. Everything was tied on because of the wind. I wished I was tied on.

The two low windbreaks made no difference, but Barry Goldman brought out his *pièce de résistance*: a large piece of blue plastic which he tied around the two windward walls. It bulged into the platform despite being braced by a wooden plank, but it held.

The boat was moored to the platform with two ropes so we didn't lose it, and the tide was coming in fast as night fell. Luminous little flashes were everywhere on the coral below in the dark. The water was now over the bottom platform and the waves were crashing through about a metre below us.

There seemed little doubt to me that the platform would not survive a good cyclone.

There has been one other similar scientific platform in the world—in the Red Sea, but there were not the same dangers of wind, wave, tide and cyclone to worry about. Barry Goldman however did not think his platform was too frail or too exposed. A man who complained about the noise of garbagemen and other people's bathrooms in Sydney, he said above the constant wind roar: 'It is a matter of relativity—to me it is not exposed, but to the average person in Sydney it might be.'

Barry said the platform was necessary because of cost efficiency. 'A boat to do the same job would cost seventy to eighty thousand dollars and the platform cost two thousand. The outer barrier is what the reef is ... not Lizard or Heron Island or A.I.M.S. [the Australian Institute of Marine Science in Townsville, Australia's $15 million prestige marine science institution]. So really this is the only research facility on the Barrier Reef.'

Barry was pretty proud of his platform. He called it his "matchbox"—which did not improve my confidence. He was planning a compressor on the roof, a permanent radio and a liferaft. The latter sounded like a good idea to me.

Barry felt that more scientists would want to use the platform (in good weather anyway) and that all the physical factors that influenced the growth of the reef could be monitored on it for the first time—wind speed and direction, wave action, water speed and direction, temperature and salinity.

When Barry blew out the lantern we went from our cosy little world to being part of the ocean.

I lay, my feet almost dangling over the edge, with the waves sweeping beneath my bed and the roar of wind and surf pounding the reef and blocking out conversation. The platform trembled like a train and shook every time our boat was slapped by another wave. I wondered how long this pugnacious little man-made structure would last, or be allowed to last.

Barry talked about the need for research—the need to know the fish populations and the predatory pattern so that no important link was taken from the reef. We had to know the periods of breeding so some areas could be protected and others opened for visitors. 'Our goal should be to know how to use without destroying—that doesn't mean to put it in a jar,' he said.

As an example, he said that if we hopped over the side and started collecting fishes seriously we would find new species of fish not yet recorded by science. But by this time I was worried more about survival than science.

At 5 a.m. it was blowing twice as hard as before. The direction had changed and the boat was thumping into a guy wire. Barry, who'd been sleeping soundly, sat straight up in bed like a man who has heard a burglar in the front room. "It's blowing now," he said, and spent ten minutes climbing up and down moving the boat around guy wires.

He decided there and then that the platform needed a couple of extra guy wires on the windward side—a good idea. Later the wind changed again and, just as I was adjusting to this weird life, there was a loud crack like a whip—and one of the guy wires disappeared. I wished I was wearing a lifejacket. The boat had hit the wire once too often. 'One down, seven to go,' I muttered to myself. But it was just light and Barry went over the side into the water to retrieve the wire, and within fifteen minutes had it back in place.

As if I needed a reminder of the power of the sea, the thick steel hook which had held the wire at the top of the platform hung above me straightened out like a ruler by the force exerted on the wire.

After breakfast, I was so happy to be leaving Australia's most precarious outpost that, after passing all the gear from a position clinging to the scaffolding, I didn't even hesitate as I leapt on to the lurching bow, feet (now very slippery from wet bird droppings) first.

THE BURNING TISSUE

I feel I can write about skin cancer with some authority. I have it. But what really burns me up is not the sun. It is the government health departments that know how skin cancer is caused, that know more than one million Australians will suffer from this disfiguring cancer, that know it is probably the most preventable of diseases—yet do nothing about it.

In fact it would not be exaggerating to say that many authorities are actively engaged in encouraging skin cancer. I have only to drive past any school in Queensland to see scores of fair-haired, blue-eyed children standing on parade under a searing Queensland sun while being addressed by the headmaster, or a politician, from the shade of a verandah.

I have only to see teachers holding classes "in the open", and schoolboys playing cricket all day with no hats—or schoolgirls at basketball—to predict, with absolute certainty, that many of these will end up as skin cancer victims. In Queensland, about one in three of them, in fact. South of the border much less. Admittedly, it will kill only about two per cent of victims, but skin cancer can be permanently disfiguring.

Every day in Queensland I see people stamped clearly in the middle of their faces as skin cancer victims: by a round patch of livid skin resembling a moon crater—the legacy of a dose of X-ray radiation used to kill the cancer and the skin surrounds. In Queensland skin cancer is like a modern day smallpox.

Other victims have liquid nitrogen (minus 196 degrees Celsius) applied to their faces under pressure. Still others have surgery.

Australia talks a lot about preventative medicine, but when one of the country's most widespread health problems is clearly preventable, no one does anything. There are no skin cancer posters at swimming pools or at beach resorts. No warnings in cricket dressing-rooms or in schools—or at least none that I have ever seen. Certainly, no one told me when I was at school of the danger of the Queensland sun on my fair skin.

I first knew there was something wrong with my skin when I found that when drying myself after a shower it hurt to rub a spot above my forehead with a towel. I used to pat this area dry. It was like a little hole in the skin. When it didn't go away I went to a specialist. 'Skin cancer,' he said.

He told me that, because skin cancer generally did not spread like other cancers, a more cosmetic approach than radiation could first be tried. Using the ultra-cold liquid nitrogen he burnt into the area. After he stopped applying it I felt a sharp burning pain. In the next few days a scab formed and fell off. I was lucky. The cancer appeared to be done away with and I was left, not with a big mark, but a barely noticeable indentation in the skin the size of the tip of a little finger.

Since then I have had a few more early spots removed which this time manifested themselves as tiny, scaly bumps. Now the nitrogen is put on under pressure so that it goes much deeper. I return every six months for a check.

I am told that skin cancer, like many other cancers, can take as long as twenty years from cause to appearance. That is why it is generally something older people suffer from. But it is starting to appear in much younger people—especially in north Queensland. My specialist recently treated a boy of ten. 'They are just getting more sun younger,' he said. 'Usually, though, it starts to show up in the twenties.'

Early treatment is very important. Those who get it badly and do nothing can be seen in the streets of Queensland with half ears or noses and pieces of cheek missing. They are paying the price of living in Queensland—where white skin is treated with scant respect by the tropical climate.

What is desperately needed in Queensland is for health departments to spend some of their money on an advertising campaign to get people to wear hats and sunscreens. Not the usual sort of government campaign with a few faded posters. For the frustrating thing about skin cancer is that once the damage has been done there is nothing you can do about that.

Maybe it's easier to sell health hazards—like alcohol and cigarettes—than health protection. But an attempt needs to be made. A former Test cricketer with skin cancer—there are plenty of those around—could tell of his experience, for example. Why keep such an important health problem a secret?

It reached a stage in Australia a few years ago where medical scientists would not even list which skin screens were the most effective. All they would say were things like "the public should use those containing paraminobenzoic acid"—whatever that might be.

Queenslanders of European descent form the largest group of whites in the world living in the tropics—yet they evolved in response to much cooler northern conditions where a pale white skin helps to more efficiently absorb vitamin D from a weaker sun.

It is reasonable therefore to assume that white-skinned Queenslanders will evolve back the other way now, and eventually become dark-skinned—though it is expected to take ten thousand years or so for any effect to become obvious.

Meanwhile, many will pay a heavy price for living in the "Sunshine State".

MY NIGHT WITH DAISY
(11 FEBRUARY 1972)

Flying into a cyclone can be unnerving—for the crew as well as the passengers. It is the only time I have seen an air hostess crying, or a pilot looking positively dishevelled.

The cyclone is due to hit Bundaberg and that is where the Fokker Friendship which I boarded in Brisbane—with some trepidation—is heading. I am amazed that the plane is almost full. Still, we are landing in Maryborough, seventy miles south, first—and if Bundaberg is under siege the plane is staying there. Not me though. If that happens, my instructions are to continue on by car.

There is a strange assortment of people on the flight. A man from the Housing Commission who has to get to Bundaberg to sort out an accommodation problem for a woman with six children; a Sydney secretary who knows nothing of the cyclone and asks me if it is always this windy in Queensland. She is flying up for a friend's wedding. On my other side is a man who has been flying for thirty hours trying to reach Bundaberg from Italy for a family re-union. Cyclone Daisy is about to stop him.

It only takes forty-five minutes to Maryborough from Brisbane, but just after everyone has finished their coffee the plane starts getting blown around. Looking out the window I know something is wrong because of the sugar cane fields below. The cane is all flat on its side—held there by the wind. The secretary says she thought it must always look like that.

I lean across the calm Italian and look up the aisle. The cockpit door is open and I look for that touch of reassurance of two pilots sitting calmly at the controls.

They are both pointing their arms in opposite directions across one another.

The air hostesses, after talking to the pilots, give individual briefings to the passengers on where to find the emergency exits. 'We just thought that while we had nothing to do while the pilot is circling we would tell the passengers personally,' the chief hostess says when I ask what is going on.

Then, suddenly, the hostesses sit down—one just opposite us. The pilot seems to be attempting to land. He is coming in as low as possible into the wind with the airstrip on our left and, just beyond it, turns left and—good grief—the strip whisks by beneath us as if tugged by some giant hand. Yet it could not have moved—it must have been us, catapulted by the wind.

The air hostess opposite is now crying. No one else is saying anything.

I can think of nothing but the last cyclone I covered—Althea in Townsville—where north Queensland nurse, Sister Steptoe, dragged a man cut down by a flying pane of glass into a public lavatory—the only building left standing in her area—and stitched up the wound on the toilet floor.

After twenty-five minutes we make a very fast landing—like a film speeded up. The head pilot, minus his cap, is one of the first off the plane. Umbrellas rip inside out immediately they are opened. In the small Maryborough airport lounge the pilot is on the phone to Brisbane telling them in no uncertain terms that he is not continuing on. He is told to get that plane out of there. The argument continues.

Cyclones, as most Queenslanders know, are very fickle things. While we were flying up from Brisbane, Daisy had changed direction and, instead of heading for Bundaberg, had turned south to hit the coast near Maryborough. The cyclone is now less than sixty miles away. It is 2 p.m.

'The flight to Bundaberg will not depart for that area but will return to Brisbane,' an announcement says.

3 p.m. Even now it is impossible to walk a straight line in the wind. Maryborough is like a ghost town. Shop windows are taped crossways with thick, brown paper and are empty of stock. There are many anxious people in this city's four thousand homes.

Throughout the night they have listened to six radio stations which have stayed open to hear Cyclone Daisy bear down closer and closer. Now it is almost here.

Their exciting ABC television movie, *Mozambique*, has been interrupted for a fifteen-minute film of what to do in a cyclone—'of special interest to the Maryborough-Bundaberg area'. It is a film Queenslanders are used to seeing on ABC TV almost every summer—together with the eerie siren that precedes each cyclone warning.

'Plan your best route of escape in case the worst happens,' they are told. 'Stay indoors, open one window away from the cyclone, remove all objects from your garden, get together a first-aid kit, buy candles and transistor batteries, get tinned food, cook everything in your freezer now, nail down loose roofing iron.'

The film instructs the family to shower, as it might be difficult to get water later. 'If your home starts to break up, stand in the doorways holding your children.'

4 p.m. Latest forecast: 'Cyclone Daisy is still sixty miles east-north-east of Maryborough moving south-west at twelve miles an hour carrying destructive winds of more than one hundred miles an hour with flood rain.'

Tree branches go as gusts increase. Maryborough is now isolated. Black Swamp Creek is over the road to the south and Pig Creek to the north. Police warn that driving in or out of Maryborough is highly dangerous.

The Police Minister, Max Hodges, goes on air: 'The emergency plan is in operation. All services are on full alert. Stay indoors because debris can injure or kill. Keep listening after the cyclone has passed. They can turn back.'

Sheets of corrugated iron start flying. The wind is strengthening and the rain is blown horizontally. The nearby coastal resort of Hervey Bay is breaking up. Trees are snapping off and buildings going. The roof is off the telephone exchange, torn away by hundred-mile-per-hour winds.

'Please limit calls, as the operators are having trouble,' a radio station says. Forty homes in the resort have already lost their roofs.

Hervey Bay seems the best story so photographer, David May, and myself and two other newsmen hire a car and attempt to drive there. We are literally skipping along until we get out of town where trees grow close to the road. One twists and snaps twelve feet up and bounces across the road ... and there are another twenty miles of tree-lined road to Hervey Bay. David May turns the car around, and now we are travelling into the wind. A big branch misses the car and two smaller ones whack into the side.

The wind is lifting the front and the car drives like a small plane, swinging right, then left. It is difficult to keep on the road, and first gear is needed to make any headway into the wind. Still, I feel reasonably safe in the car—until I see a sheet of roofing iron from a house that loses its front verandah fly through the air and spear into the roof of a parked car. It goes straight through into the back seat. In our car that's exactly where I'm sitting.

We decide to set ourselves up in a motel—where we can listen to the radio, watch the TV and telephone our stories. It is a good set-up and I lean back, cup of tea in hand. Then a large pine tree falls and we have no lights, no radio, no TV. No information.

The only thing to do is to make a run for the police station—and that involves jumping power lines. I am tempted to test them to see if they are live.

From the police station to the post office public telephones is only a block—but I note there is no one else on the streets. It is always comforting to see someone else.

The cyclone is passing to the east of the town, but eighty- to ninety-mile-per-hour winds in Maryborough send trees crashing through power lines. Elderly residents huddle in doorways in the dark—many lose their radio and TV communication with the electricity. Then they lose their phones.

Windows splinter in the gusts, leaving the wind to rip into homes—the reason for opening a window on the other side to the cyclone. Radio broadcasts warn of flying roofing iron. In Hervey Bay they say a two-thousand-gallon water tank spins at forty-five miles per hour up a roadway and the fence of the football ground has disintegrated.

It is the height of the cyclone in Maryborough. A Golden Fleece sign sails up the road and disappears. A house verandah crashes. Roofing iron smashes shop windows. Power lines are down everywhere. Most of the city is blacked out.

1 a.m. Saturday: It is frightening in a cyclone. It is frightening to see the power of the wind. All the time it makes a diabolical howl.

8 a.m.: Maryborough Airport is open but visitors are still stranded. Cyclone Daisy is near Brisbane and now Brisbane Airport is closed.

10 a.m.: The radios come on. The sun comes out. Streets echo to hammering. Yellow-helmeted linesmen swing from poles, pulling big wires in line. Men chop and clean the prone trees.

A man visiting his mother's home picks a wire off the gate. Two hours of respiration fail to save him. He is the only known death in this area from Daisy ... a small cyclone by Queensland standards.

JAWS FEELING THE PINCH

Had the giant white pointer of *Jaws* come cruising off the Gold Coast past Surfers Paradise looking for a tasty human morsel he would almost certainly have been in for a big surprise. For just beyond the waves along this stretch of golden beaches are twelve separate two-hundred-metre-long braided nylon cord shark net traps. These run more or less parallel to the beaches, dangling five metres down to near the bottom, about a kilometre off shore. The holes in the nets are only twenty-five centimetres across and they hang loosely in a diamond shape awaiting their deadly foe ... if they were tight the sharks would burst right through.

Many a *Jaws*-type white pointer in fact has come to grief in these nets off Queensland's Gold Coast and other netted beaches. In Queensland these sharks are also called the "White Death" because they are proven man-eaters—and they have even been known to make several big holes in the state's net traps. But even the largest of sharks is as good as dead if he so much as touches one of these loosely hanging nets. Once against the net, the struggling shark becomes hopelessly tied up and, in effect, drowns. For a shark, unlike other fish, must have water constantly moving over its gills to collect oxygen. That is why sharks are always on the move ... a deadly wandering which makes them more dangerous, but also more vulnerable to a set net.

These toothy predators also have to resist lovely bloody chunks of meat suspended from buoys out beyond the breakers. Inside each irresistible mouthful is a giant Norwegian shark hook. Once he has swallowed that the shark is attached to a steel trace with more than a tonne breaking strain.

Since shark meshing was first introduced in Queensland in the 1962-63 holiday season no fewer than 17,151 sharks have been captured and killed. In that time the programme has been extended up the coast as far north as Cairns to the most popular beaches. Fifty-three Queensland beaches have traps for the hungry shark, consisting of 51 nets and 141 lines. Queensland meshes more beaches and catches more sharks than anywhere else in the world. In Australia the white pointer is in fact found mostly in southern Queensland and South Australia. Four of the world shark records for game fishing are now held for white death sharks caught in Queensland.

What makes them so terrifying, locals say, is the big dark eye which gives a look of staring and apparent intelligence, of ferocity and constant watchfulness. As Queensland shark expert Peter Goadby said: 'If one were superstitious it would be easy to believe that the white death is guided by evil supernatural spirits as the fables sometimes say. A white shark attacking resembles a silent super-fortress with its graceful pectoral fins and effortless, lithe manoeuvring. The silence ends when it attacks. Then, if its head is out of the water, the growls and ripping sounds are never forgotten.'

They can grow to at least a tonne and a half and up to twelve metres long. A recently extinct giant species of the white shark had teeth fifteen centimetres long and is thought to have grown to twenty-four metres in some cases. Peter Benchley, the author of *Jaws*, ponders if this fish might still exist in the ocean depths, and says it would resemble 'a locomotive with a mouth full of butcher's knives'.

To try to keep such monsters away from hapless swimmers the Queensland government spends almost a quarter of a million dollars a year.

The record shows that since the first recorded shark attack in Queensland in 1919 there have been forty-four attacks resulting in twenty-seven deaths. This excludes such mystery cases as the two Department of Harbours and Marine officers whose boat was found without them. But from the ripped clothing floating in the water many experts assumed they were taken by a shark. Significantly, all of the twenty-seven deaths, except one, occurred before 1962 (when shark meshing first started)—and the later fatality was at a beach where there was no shark meshing.

Just prior to the introduction of the nets, there were several horrifying shark attacks on Queensland's tourist beaches. In December 1961, for example, three people were attacked by sharks, two fatally. A week before Christmas—approaching the peak of the holiday season—a young man died at Noosa after having his left leg torn off in shallow water. Ten days later in north Queensland a woman lost a leg and both arms, and the man she was with lost his right arm, as they fought a big shark. The woman died. It was after these attacks that meshing was introduced.

Since then the average size of the sharks taken has decreased—and so has the number. The first season of meshing at the Gold Coast lasted only seven months and netted 526 man-eaters. After that the season was increased to ten and a half months but that figure has never again been approached. During the 1975 season it had fallen to 262. But the sharks are still there—beyond the meshing. The prawners say that out at the ten fathom mark they are still pestered by sharks all the time. When they lift the prawn nets up the sharks still attack, and are always around the boats. Meshing is not infallible and it is prudent to avoid swimming early or late in the day, or in murky water. Overcast weather has also been associated with shark attacks.

Because of the huge meshing programme much has been learned about the shark, which has remained relatively unchanged for almost two hundred million years. They were the first animals in the world to have teeth. Man, the experts say, followed the lead of the sharks.

The mesh nets now are down twenty-four hours a day seven days a week throughout the swimming season, and contractors service them every other day to remove dead or live sharks. A live shark is shot before being handled or winched up in the air. They are just too dangerous to tangle with. When they are hauled on board the sharks are measured, identified for sex, and the stomach contents examined. A complete record is kept for scientific purposes. The Queensland programme has shown that tiger sharks are predators of sea snakes, and it has proved that sharks travel up coastal rivers because flying foxes, which inhabit the banks of these rivers, have been found in the stomachs of sharks. Tiger sharks—known scavengers—have been found with tin cans inside them, and near Mackay a tiger shark had the hooves of a goat in its stomach.

The longest shark caught at a Queensland beach was a five-metre tiger and the heaviest was a white pointer which weighed so much the vessel could not winch it aboard and had to tow it to a wharf and use a mobile crane. It weighed an estimated one and a half tonnes. In another incident a huge white pointer attacked a boat leaving two teeth embedded in the hull.

Swimmers, therefore, can now be thankful that there's more between them and "Jaws" than a flimsy bathing costume.

FLOODED WITH WARNINGS

On three successive Sundays in 1819 the early Australian settlers—at least those who went to church—were warned of the dangers of flooding posed by the volatile east coast rivers. In an order dated 5 March 1819, Governor Lachlan Macquarie warned of the 'dreadful inundations' that could ensue from such rivers. He criticized new settlers for their 'wilful and wayward habit of placing their residences within the reach of the floods, as if putting at defiance that impetuous element which it is not for man to contend with'. It was, he wrote, not within the reach of human foresight 'to guard against the baneful recurrence of such awful visitations'.

Yet today, seven generations later, Australians are still making the same mistakes, still wilfully and waywardly living in the path of future floods.

Governor Macquarie insisted his order be read at every church and chapel in Australia for three successive Sundays, so important did he believe the information to be. Yet even the disastrous Brisbane flood of Australia Day 1974—in terms of economic loss the most devastating in the country's history—brought little or no change in regulations and attitudes.

Those in low lying areas of Brisbane, Ipswich, Lismore, Maitland, Grafton, Gunnedah, Narrabri, Wee Waa, Gympie, Moree, and the Yarra Valley might well contemplate what Governor Macquarie thought of people who settled next to flood prone rivers: 'Those who, notwithstanding, shall perversely neglect the present admonition and exhortation to their own benefit, must be considered wilfully and obstinately blind to their true interests and undeserving any future indulgences.'

It was not until 1975 that the Housing and Research Branch in the Australian government's Department of Housing and Construction produced a publication explaining about building in flood prone areas, and drew up suggested flood regulations for existing council building by-laws. The report pointed out something that people in Brisbane learned to their detriment in 1974—that dams, reservoirs and levees could never eliminate floods and, in fact, led the community to be overly optimistic of the flood protection provided. 'The provision of even a degree of flood prevention invites continued, and perhaps even increased, use of the protected area: people tend to confuse a degree of protection with complete protection', the report said.

This was particularly the case with Brisbane where the popular belief was that, as there had been no great flood since the building of the Somerset dam, flooding had been eliminated. But some at least knew of the risk. As early as 1971 the Queensland government was warned by its own experts that Brisbane and Ipswich faced the certainty of a devastating flood. The warning predictions were made in a 136-page report prepared by the state government's Co-ordinator-General's Department. It proved extremely accurate and included such phrases as 'enormous damage', 'unjustified complacency', and 'possible tragedy'. The report even went so far as to recommend that 'information of the flood risk from the Brisbane River in various areas being developed, or subject to development, be released'. It added that 'this might be done in the form of a plan showing the probability of flooding'.

Yet nothing was done. For two more years people and developers were allowed to go on building homes which authorities knew were in the path of an inevitable flood.

The report estimated that 'the damage from a major flood could amount to at least $85 million'—not far off the damage estimate for the Australia Day flood. And it added prophetically: 'The major part of the damage from flooding would be to private property since building has been permitted in areas known to have a high flood risk.'

But, warnings or no warnings, it was a certainty that Brisbane would get a massive flood. In fact, although fourteen thousand houses were inundated, thousands of people evacuated and all but two main roads cut in the biggest flood of the century, the 1974 flood was by no means as bad as could be expected to occur, sooner or later.

Between 1840 and 1900 three much bigger floods hit Brisbane and another three of equal size gushed through the city. Yet Brisbane was lulled into a false sense of security this century because until Cyclone Wanda struck in 1974 there had been nothing of real note except the 1931 flood when the water in the Brisbane River registered about 4.4 metres above sea level. So Brisbane people built closer and closer to the river and its creeks. The only restriction by the Brisbane City Council had been to stop building below the 1931 flood level.

In January 1974 the Brisbane River rose almost two and a half metres above the 1931 level, hurling water into homes previously considered (at least this century) as safe. One of the worst hit suburbs was Jindalee, a picturesque new middle-class development on the banks of the normally placid river.

Literally overnight, the river became a swollen torrent. You could hear it from a hundred metres away rushing past, tossing forty-four gallon drums up and down like tiny corks and ripping giant ships from their moorings. The muddy water reached the tenth row of seats at the famous Milton tennis courts, and made towering home unit blocks on the river at St Lucia part of the river. Swirling water flooded the basements and first floors of at least a third of the buildings in the city centre. Businessmen in swimming togs swam into city offices and moved safes and computers to higher floors as the river slowly spread out into the city. A sandbag wall was built around the telephone exchange and a bank vault.

Imagine though what the damage would have been like if it had been as bad as, say, the 1893 flood. In that flood the present site of Queensland University was under water and a steamer took a short cut across the area to Oxley. The two bridges across the river, the Indooroopilly railway bridge and the old Victoria Bridge, were washed away. Queen Street was under water. Four separate cyclones about the same size as Wanda inundated the Brisbane area over a month in 1893. In twenty-four hours Brisbane received an unbelievable Australian record rainfall of 35 inches 71 points (907 millimetres), compared with the fall of 14 inches (355 millimetres) which set off the flood in 1974. In three days during the 1893 flood 72 inches (1,829 millimetres) fell. On February 5 the Brisbane River reached its highest-ever level of 9.5 metres—3 metres above the 1974 flood—and, though it was then a very small city, ten thousand families were given assistance. A fortnight later, after the flood had gone, the Brisbane River showed its perverseness when a fourth cyclone struck and another flood, almost as big, swept downstream.

If these floods occurred today they would be devastating. In 1893 many areas near rivers had not been built on. As it was, the Department of Science official report on the 1974 flood estimated damage at $200 million. Twelve people were drowned and an additional two died as a direct result of the floods. Several elderly people suffered fatal heart attacks while being evacuated from their flood ravaged homes, and a two-year-old child was swept from his father's arms and drowned in Oxley Creek near the Brisbane suburb of Inala. The report said the flood also had a heavy sociological impact on the community. In some metropolitan creek-side suburbs residents returned to their homes early and commenced cleaning up only to find themselves flooded out again soon after. Some people were permanently affected, both physically and mentally, by the shock of the flood and its aftermath.

The 1974 Brisbane flood was so relentless that although it commenced on the night of January 25 it did not reach its peak until January 29 and did not subside until January 31. And out of the mud, debris and stench left by the flood a terrible fact emerged: only about one per cent of the victims received any insurance payout for their badly damaged houses, even though they believed they were covered by their "storm and tempest" policies.

A check with private and state insurance companies showed that the great majority of people insured their houses for "storm and tempest"—but this did not cover a cyclonic flood. "Storm and tempest", in fact, does not even cover rain damage to homes—but 50 per cent of the public take out a separate rain cover. "Storm and tempest" means a violent atmospheric disturbance accompanied by high wind or rain, snow or hail. But it does not mean persistent bad weather or heavy rain or persistent rain by itself. Additional rain insurance covers only 'water falling from the sky in the form of rain until such time as it reaches the ground and falls on the building insured'.

Cyclone Wanda certainly filled the bill of 'a violent atmospheric disturbance accompanied by high winds and rain'. But a completely separate policy was needed for flood insurance, even if the damage resulted from that same atmospheric disturbance. And, according to insurance industry sources, this was not generally offered to householders unless they specifically asked for it.

'People who believe they don't live in a flood area tend to get very excited if you ask them if they want flood insurance. It's plain bad PR,' said one insurance man.

Some people, of course, received government aid but that was minimal. Premier Bjelke-Petersen said relief would be given only to those 'in necessitous circumstances'. Those who had financial resources were expected 'to look to the means at their disposal. The government cannot be expected to refurnish homes but only to ensure the people at least have the essentials.'

In the wake of the flood a sort of bitter humour developed, and people were quick to realize what the effect on real estate values would be. The sign outside a once-elegant brick home in exclusive Cromarty Street, Kenmore read: 'For Sale. Price 1 dozen XXXX and a clean glass. Features: Holds 788,000 gallons, no fridge, muddy pool.'

At St Lucia, another pleasant riverside Brisbane suburb, a sign above a flooded street read: 'St Lucia water canal development. Prestige apartments. No fishing.' Farther away from the river there was another FOR SALE sign: 'Riverside views on certain occasions'.

These were manifestations of the new real estate mood in Brisbane—a mood which threw the local real estate market into confusion and altered the basis for all subsequent valuations. Once Brisbane people had competed fiercely for riverside blocks; then suddenly nobody wanted to know about them. Yet there was also a feeling that the great flood would soon be forgotten. As one real estate agent said: 'People have been living on the side of Vesuvius for two thousand years.'

A well-known Brisbane solicitor who got his wife and kids and $50,000 worth of paintings out in his Mercedes before his riverside mansion went under caused a lot of laughs at a "flood party" by maintaining he was going to buy the highest block of land in Brisbane. 'You see those red lights,' he said, pointing to the TV towers on top of Brisbane's Mount Coot-tha. 'Well that's where I'm building.' But on sober reflection he decided he would move back to the riverside for a few years 'and sell to a southerner'. He was not alone in such thoughts.

But those who did sell their stinking houses had to take a quick loss. Within days of the flood, advertisements began appearing in local papers: 'Flood victims. Will pay cash today. $14,000 to $16,000 for a 3-brm home.' And: 'Flood-affected homes wanted to buy. Development company will buy your flood-damaged home. Prompt cash payment.'

By 1979 real estate agents said it was relatively easy to sell houses that were flooded. More flooded houses were sold in 1976 than in the previous two years combined. Although at that stage those that had been flooded were still being sold at a discount, and the more costly the house the greater the percentage of the discount. As time goes on however the discount is gradually lessening. And each year government complacency grows.

Now Brisbane awaits the completion of the Wivenhoe Dam, most people believing, with the state government, that it will eliminate bad floods. It won't. Floods as bad as 1974 will still be possible. After all they've been occurring for thousands of years in the Brisbane area. On 28 September 1824, John Oxley noted, after exploring the Brisbane River, that there was evidence of immense flooding—'although "flood" would be too weak an expression to use for a collection of water rising to the height (full 50 feet) which the appearance of the shore here renders probable'. To his amazement he saw flood-deposited debris high up in riverbank trees.

Aboriginal legends describe huge inundations by rivers, and all along the eastern coast the Aborigines told early settlers of great floods that had occurred back in the dreamtime. Some of their stories in fact concerned floods of such magnitude that the settlers dismissed them as nothing more than legends.

A penal colony was established at Moreton Bay in 1824 and the following year it was moved from the Bay to the banks of the flood-prone Brisbane River. Evidently those responsible for the site of the colony had not attended church in 1819 and so missed Governor Macquarie's dire warning of 'dreadful inundations'. And many good citizens of Brisbane, it seems, have been ignoring such warnings ever since.

COPPING THE RAW PRAWN

A FAIR COW OF A TURNOUT

In October 1972 three Aborigines were convicted in the District Court at Charleville in western Queensland of killing a cow with intent to steal meat from the carcass. The court was told that the sight of one of the men had started to fail six months before the offence. He could not see with his left eye and had only minor sight in his right eye. He was on an invalid pension.

The man, Frederick Lawton, aged thirty-three, was living with and supporting his wife and seven children aged from six months to eleven years. He had no previous convictions.

Another accused, Archie Fraser, a forty-three-year-old railway fettler, was supporting his de facto wife and eight children plus two children of his de facto daughter. He had not previously been convicted of a similar offence.

The third man, Richard Floyd Fraser, eighteen years old and unemployed, had only one previous conviction—for stealing poultry worth twenty dollars. He was the one who shot the cow.

Each of the men claimed he was to some degree affected by alcohol at the time of the offence. All pleaded guilty.

The crown prosecutor told the court that the offence was considered to be prevalent, but there were not many convictions for it.

Judge McCracken asked the men, who were not legally represented, 'You do not disagree with what the crown prosecutor said, that this offence is committed frequently out here?'

Archie Fraser: 'I don't think so, no.'

Judge McCracken: 'Is there anything else you want to say, any of you?'

There was no reply.

Passing sentence, Judge McCracken said: 'So far as Lawton is concerned, the state is supporting him. So, if he went to prison, the state would continue supporting his family. The same applies to Archie Fraser.'

He sentenced the three men to eighteen months' gaol and said they should be considered for parole after six months.

Early in 1973 the case was taken to the State Court of Criminal Appeal, for an appeal on the grounds that the sentence was manifestly excessive. The facts of the case were put before the chief justice, Mr Justice Hanger, Mr Justice Wanstall and Mr Justice Stable.

The chief justice said, in his judgment, that he noticed that Fraser had not disagreed with the crown prosecutor's statement that the offence was prevalent.

'I think it is common knowledge that the offence in relation to dealing with cattle which do not belong to persons is a prevalent one in the district of Charleville,' Mr Justice Hanger said. 'In the circumstances I think the learned trial judge was quite justified in imposing the sentence which he did. I have no hesitation in saying that I do not think it is manifestly excessive. In fact I think if there were any error in it at all it was on the light side.'

Mr Justice Hanger said he could see no reason for saying that even with regard to the youngest of the three, who was eighteen, the sentence was manifestly excessive. He dismissed the appeal. The other judges agreed.

Thus, three Aborigines—an almost blind invalid pensioner with seven young children, a man with ten children to look after and an eighteen-year-old youth—failed in their appeal against an eighteen-month sentence for killing a cow ... a cow they had killed for food.

In August 1973 in another western Queensland town, this time Roma, a man pleaded guilty to a charge of having stolen fourteen calves worth an average of $40 each—a total of $560. This time it was a white man, Neville Thomas Smith, property manager, married, with five children. And this time the stolen property was for sale—the court was told the calves were taken to Dalby to be sold. Again, evidence was given as to the prevalence of the offence. The officer-in-charge of Roma stock squad, Detective Sergeant Keith Kinlin, told the court stock thefts in the year to last June were valued at $258,946—almost double the previous year. Only $6,420 worth of stock was recovered.

Judge Carter in the Roma District Court gaoled Smith for nine months.

NOTHING MUCH COOKING IN COOKTOWN

A forgotten Queensland town has threatened to swing its only armament—a nineteenth century cannon—around to point towards Brisbane and Canberra. For the residents of Queensland's northernmost east coast town, Cooktown, more than two thousand kilometres from Brisbane, believe Australia has forgotten them and ignored their many unusual problems. They believe that governments in the southern half of the continent—including Brisbane—have no idea what Cooktown is up against.

The locals have worked out, for example, that there is more bitumen roadway on the Sydney Harbour Bridge and its approaches than in their entire 125,000 square kilometre shire. That's right, less than 13 kilometres of bitumen road. Their railway line was closed about twenty years ago, and the dirt road from Cairns to Cooktown travels a circuitous 340 kilometres instead of 160 kilometres in a straight line. And mail takes four days to get out of Cooktown to Cairns. Australia built its first atomic research station before Cooktown got electricity, and there was no town water until 1971.

They have been told they can't have a bitumen road to Cairns because it would cost many millions—about as much in fact as the short stretch of freeway between Sydney and Wollongong. Agitation began in earnest in July 1975 when Cooktown lost its weekly boat run from Cairns—a service that has kept the town going for fifty years. For in the wet the road link with Cairns is closed for months at a time. So the town was looking forward to summers with little fresh milk, few vegetables and even fewer tourists. And what if they were wiped out by a cyclone? It has happened twice before this century.

Cooktown though was not always a forgotten town. In the late nineteenth century the town became an Eldorado, with forty thousand people, half of them Chinese, searching for gold. There were four newspapers in those days, one of them Chinese. Things were booming then. Mail came in nearly every day from all over the globe. You could walk down to the wharf any hour of the day and catch a clipper or a square rigger from Brisbane, Sydney, San Francisco, London or Hong Kong. After all, Cooktown was frequently the first international port of call in Australia for the world shipping lines. At that time the capacious harbour was forested with masts flying the ensigns of every nation.

But the gold ran out. The miners started leaving, although according to the Cooktown storekeeper, Jim Curran, the fastest exodus was made by 'the fickle politicians' because there were other votes to attract from southern populations. A cyclone decimated Cooktown in 1907, and another one in 1949 nearly finished off the town.

Jim Curran wrote a long and sharply pointed letter to Premier Bjelke-Petersen in 1975: 'Sir, Cape York has surrendered its gold, its tin, its cedar forests and now its bauxite to the rest of the nation for over a century. Can't we please have some of it back in bridges and bitumen.'

The Cooktown storekeeper reminded the premier to write his reply on a Thursday to catch the weekly mail to Cooktown. And added: 'Oh, incidentally, about that old cannon sent us late last century. We still have it. It sits placidly on the banks of the Endeavour River facing towards the harbour mouth. It is true a sinister element in our community advocates swinging it round 180 degrees, but our committee assures you that no such posture of militancy will be encouraged—at this juncture.'

BEENLEIGH'S POWERFUL SPIRIT

Driving into a town which is on cholera alert is not the ideal assignment so, to get my bearings when I reached Beenleigh, I stopped in at one of the town's three hotels and ordered a scotch and water. That was my first mistake.

The order attracted incredulous looks along the bar and one gentleman leaned across: 'You from out of town mate,' he said. 'Nobody is drinking water here unless they see it boiled with their own eyes.'

I changed my order to ginger ale and moved further along the bar where another gentleman told me I should try the new local drink. I knew he must be referring to the famous Beenleigh rum but, weakened by my close call with cholera, I came in spinner: 'What drink's that?'—'Rum and cholera' he announced with glee and much laughter from his mates.

Another chap picked an imaginary germ off my shoulder, put it on the bar and hit it hard with his hand. 'Got ya,' he said. The jokes were a defence mechanism, I supposed. But, moving to another hotel, I ran into a group of men who blamed the media for 'sensationalism' in reporting the cholera outbreak. 'We have total confidence in the health authorities for the way they got on to it. There has been no panic—all the panic has been everywhere but here.' The others nodded agreement, but a man further up the bar annoyed them by yelling out: 'There are no worries, I still drink the water.'

One of the group explained that the township had not panicked because no one knew the couple from the caravan park who'd been taken to hospital. 'They are faceless people and Beenleigh is still a close-knit town. If it had been a local identity that would have caused panic. Imagine what that would have caused. But the woman is unknown, an outcast, they don't know her here and so they don't really care.'

The general consensus in the bar was that the cholera must have come from Canungra army camp. 'They say there have been no foreigners, like Indonesians, there recently but we have been told that cholera can live where it is deposited by humans for three years,' one man said. Some drinkers were unhappy that people around Australia might think their town dirty—and one was upset that cameramen from Brisbane had filmed the older end of town.

The town put on a pretty brave face in the bars, but in the lounge rooms of the wooden houses in this small town—which is now bypassed by the four-lane highway to the Gold Coast—there was profound concern. Mrs Pam Radke greeted me with a big smile at her front door and, not knowing I had just eaten a Beenleigh burger from a snack bar, proceeded to tell me of the dangers of eating food prepared by others, and how a local doctor warned against this at a club meeting. People boiled their water and disinfected their hands before touching food.

'We know it's serious and we are taking all precautions here too. In this house you name it and it's boiled,' Mrs Radke said. 'I have told my boys not to buy food prepared in this area.' My hamburger rumbled suspiciously.

Her son Bob, who works in Brisbane as a washing machine repairman, said he had a problem going to work each day from a cholera area. 'I don't touch their cutlery at work anymore. They bought me my own plastic cup and I now have a plastic spoon, fork and knife wrapped in plastic.' On the mug, he inscribed his name ... and a skull and crossbones.

'People answer the phone here now and say things like "Hello, Cholera City"—it's all relieving the tension.' Mrs Radke was even boiling the water for the dog. 'That might sound funny but he is also getting only canned food.'

Another resident, Mrs Dot Hamilton, said people were confused and too many questions on what they should do had been left unanswered. She showed me a leaflet handed out at a meeting on the cholera scare in the town. With the classic understatement of the bureaucracy—like the local swimming pool which bears the sign 'Closed Till Further Notice'—the leaflet began: 'A public health problem has arisen in your area'. It warned that cholera could be passed on from food or water, by flies or through hand contamination and could take up to five days for symptoms to appear.

What Beenleigh people found hardest to understand was why the state government health people waited four days to announce that the cholera case was from Beenleigh. 'They knew of the cholera case on Monday and said she was from the outer southern side of Brisbane,' said Mrs Hamilton. 'Then on Thursday we were shocked to find it was Beenleigh—and we had been drinking that cholera water unboiled all week. I only found out when I just happened to turn the TV on and saw a local councillor and thought "What's he doing on TV?" Admittedly they didn't want to scare people but we had to be told eventually.'

The main street of Beenleigh was not as busy as usual as I headed out of town after declining a parting offer of a biscuit and cup of tea. I felt I had taken enough risks for one day.

BOOTHLESS IN BEDOURIE

An entire outback Queensland town never got a vote in the 1975 federal election because it was too far away from the rest of Australia. The town was Bedourie, which is so isolated that its location is invariably given as: '120 miles north of Birdsville'.

A combination of circumstances led to the town losing its voice in the wilderness. The Canberra government decided after the May 1974 poll to eliminate a number of voting booths with a small number of voters as an economy measure—and Bedourie, with about forty voters, was one of the first to go. In mid 1975 the family that had given Bedourie a road mail service for fifty years gave it away because of rising costs in the west. Bedourie then had to rely on a plane service for mail once a fortnight.

'None of us had a chance to vote,' said Jean Smith, mother of the licensee of the town's only hotel, The Royal. 'It was not only the Bedourie people who missed out but the district all around, I should imagine forty or fifty of us in all. Of course there are not as many now as there used to be. We tried to get postal votes but if we write a letter with a fortnightly service it takes a month to get a reply ... and then we can't reply for another fortnight. We have just about lost interest in writing at all. I can't understand why we couldn't have a booth. I suppose we must blame the people who were in power in Canberra—they have given us a bad spin. I think they knew how we would vote and so didn't want us to have a vote. Anyway that's the way I look at it.'

Mrs Smith has reared four sons and has another at school. She says she has always had it tough but has never heard of Australians missing their vote before. 'I was reared on the Birdsville Track—it was a place called Ooroowilanie—until I was seventeen. There was just us there. We came up there on a horse and buggy in 1926.'

Bedourie, of course, has no television and no longer gets any papers. 'The pilot brought one for us from Adelaide recently. They used to let the papers off at Birdsville and they came from there but it is a bit awkward apparently now. Anyway we couldn't afford them. We are about nine hundred or a thousand miles from Brisbane and, although we are in Queensland, just a little bit closer to Adelaide.'

Even the public phone in Bedourie has just been cut. 'All we got was a notification from the PMG and there was no reason at all. They just did it,' she said.

Mrs Smith sounded a bit bewildered by it all. She said that on voting day some people planned to drive the 391-kilometre return trip to Boulia to vote but it rained.

'Everyone just sat around all day and that night they listened to the radio and I suppose you could say there was a lot of cheering.'

THE OLD RAZZIE DAZZLE

The Queensland police inspector, a uniformed sergeant and a civilian were having trouble communicating—and the sergeant was plainly nonplussed by the conversation.

Sergeant: The old blacks are still playing up?

Inspector: The blacks ...

Sergeant: Hey?

Inspector: Yeah, um, yeah.

The conversation was to become more and more disjointed but what the police sergeant and the civilian didn't know was that the conversation was being recorded—only the inspector was aware of this. It was being tape recorded for use as evidence in court. The conversation suddenly swung back on to Aborigines.

Sergeant: Want a bloody good waddy over their nut.

Inspector: Orh they have done the wrong thing by those people you know.

Sergeant: (puzzled by his superior's attitude): What?

Inspector: They've done the wrong thing by those people.

Sergeant: What, by the blacks?

Inspector: Yeah.

Civilian: Ha, ha, ha.

Sergeant: Didn't kill enough of the buggers.

Inspector: No, no, encouraging them round to grog around the town, to drink grog.

Sergeant: Yeah, well who encourages them?

Inspector: Well, some from, some ... some of the political parties.

Sergeant: I don't think it would require such bloody encouraging.

Inspector (nervously): Ha, ha, ha.

Sergeant: Hey?

Inspector: Ha ha.

Sergeant: Bloody ...

This weird conversation was kept for posterity in the report of the criminal law inquiry in Queensland. This report, after being studied by a three-man state government committee including the police commissioner, Terry Lewis, was then shelved by the government, despite the report's important recommendations.

The strange exchange quoted was presented in the report as an example of 'the problems of protecting individuals from undue pressure in investigations and interrogations of offences by police officers'. The report said: 'In the case of Aborigines there were sad stories ranging from allegations of misunderstanding down to frank brutality.'

The conversation between the inspector of police, the uniformed sergeant and the civilian was tape recorded and later introduced as evidence in the course of proceedings in the magistrates court. It went on:

Inspector: Ha, ha, ha, that's pretty right Jack. They like that—bright lights and a bottle of plonk, they're pretty right.

Silence.

Inspector: Um.

Civilian: See them drunk early, about eight o'clock in the morning ...

Inspector: Yeah.

Civilian: Toddling down the street.

Sergeant: Oh, the good old days are gone with the blacks. You can't give them a bloody razzle dazzle like you used to be able to.

Inspector: No.

THE SPORTING LIFE

GAMBLING WITH SUCCESS

It was 1966 and the end of an eight-month English winter when the phone rang, long distance from Nice, on the French Riviera. It was my eternally optimistic mate from Annerley Junction, Brisbane—tennis player Ken Fletcher. At the Nice casino he had won a bundle of French francs, a VW station wagon (from an American playing the same table) and a sparkling diamond bracelet (from the Oriental gentleman at his other elbow). The sun was shining in Nice, he said, there was a ticket waiting for me at London's Heathrow airport, and we could drive over to Monte Carlo together for the tennis tournament where he had been booked into a hotel room. I could share the room with him.

There were no seats available on the Nice flight the next morning but I went to the airport anyway and got a seat when someone didn't turn up.

It was disappointing that Fletch, as everyone called him, had lost in the first round of each of the southern French tournaments because I knew just how good he was as a tennis player. But that was Kenny Fletcher. If he wanted to win he could—if he didn't, anyone could beat him. The previous summer when a young Australian beat him in London the youth shook hands at the net and said: 'Gee, Fletch, now I will get into Wimbledon without qualifying because I can put on my entry form that I beat Ken Fletcher.'

'Every roughie in the world's got that on his form,' said Fletcher, whose speech was laced with horse racing terminology.

Before agreeing to get on the plane I had made him promise he would try to win the Monte Carlo tournament so I could enjoy the tennis as well as the nightlife. I knew he could win if he put his mind to it. (And a few months later he and John Newcombe won the Wimbledon men's doubles—the fourth year in a row Fletcher had made the final.) But most of the time he didn't use the ability he had. Some theorized it was because when he was young he could beat everybody he played—except one kid from the bush who was two years older, a bloke called Rod Laver. But others were closer to the truth when they said that Fletcher enjoyed life too much. As a journalist once wrote of Fletcher: 'They say that opportunity knocks only once: in Ken Fletcher's case it has almost battered down the door.'

Just how much he enjoyed life became obvious not long after the plane touched down. I walked out of immigration and customs to see, leaning on the VW, the usual cheerful Fletch, as always looking boyish with his short fair hair brushed straight back and the clear blue eyes that could read the destination label of a tram down the length of Queen Street.

We shook hands and he said: 'I've still got the car, got any money for petrol?' He had lost the money and the bracelet the previous night, but still held on to ownership of the car—a deed signed by both parties at the roulette wheel on a white dinner napkin.

It did not seem a very auspicious start. But Fletch was not to be daunted: all the way through the rock tunnels to Monte Carlo he sang: 'I'm the man who broke the bank in Monte Carlo.'

We moved into room 37 at the Hotel Europa and Fletch took me down to show me a typical South of France beach. Two old Gold Coast boys, we stood and looked at the rocky beach with no waves and laughed till our sides hurt. Then we went back to the room where we played his favourite record at the time, Dean Martin singing 'Goin' Back to Houston, Houston, Houston'—and we sang along 'Brisbane, Brisbane, Brisbane'.

After a night out at the cabaret and the casino it took the room phone many rings to wake us. It was the tennis club secretary. Monsieur Fletcher was due to play Daniel Contet, the French clay champion, at 11 a.m. It was now 12.30. They gave him five minutes to get there.

The wealthy tennis club had three tiers of red clay tennis courts overlooking the blue Med. I surprised some French officials by predicting Fletcher would win the tournament, but Fletch lost the first set. Concerned that this would be the end of my tennis enjoyment, I yelled out to remind him of his promise.

'Right oh, I'll beat him two and three,' he said, and went on to win 6-3 and 6-2.

That night, dressed in the white sports coat he used to wear so often, Fletcher gained entrance to the exclusive private club at the back of the casino above the cabaret. We were in a party with a fellow he coached occasionally—Peter Acropolis—a nephew of Onassis. Jackie Kennedy's sister, Princess Lee Radziwell, was in the party which bet with big white 1,000 franc chips.

While Fletch and I worked on perfecting a winning system with the Monte Carlo tournament expenses he had just collected, Peter backed number 11 every time—and when it came up at 35 to 1 he would bang the table and shout 'Bravo' at the top of his voice. A pretty French blonde in the party who also was some sort of princess swore clearly and concisely every time her number failed to come up.

There were all sorts of rorts being pulled in that casino—as Fletch so ably pointed out. But the best was by the two beautiful girls at a crowded table who very kindly helped place the big chips of a very rich American ... for he couldn't reach over them, and he was happy to have an excuse to talk to them. Finally, he had a huge win. The thirty-five thousand francs were pushed across the table by the chief croupier from his central high seat which gave him complete say over every dispute at the table. The girls swept the money into their open handbags and smiled at the American. He yelled at the chief croupier that the money was his and that it had better be handed over. The chief croupier threatened him with eviction by the casino's numerous henchmen, saying: 'Monsieur, madame place the bet.'

In the following days of the tournament Fletcher beat Marty Riessen from the U.S., some South American star Fletch called 'the Road Runner' because he chased and returned impossible shots, and then Italian champion Pietrangali in a hard fought match. A true Annerley Junction boy, when the going got tough and hot he ignored the gold fountains by the side of the court and drank out of the green hose down the back.

At 4 a.m. each day we came out of the elegant private casino with more money than when we entered. By Friday Fletcher had won his way into the final, and was starring in a high society concert that night. He still faced the problem of getting the left-hand-drive car with German number plates into England with only a dinner napkin to prove ownership. He was also searching for the wily gentleman who had taken the diamond bracelet to have it valued. And all this tennis, he complained, was making him tired.

He was playing the world's best clay court player, Manuel Santana, in the Saturday final. But I couldn't stay for that because I had stories to write in London about things that were, editors thought, more interesting than a summer vacation with Fletch in Monte Carlo.

At the concert on Friday night they had written a special song for Fletch to sing to the tune of 'Mañana Mañana' accompanied by two cabaret girls. The chorus went:

Oh I'd like to be a champion
And win the tennis crown–
If only I could somehow learn
To play it lying down.

Not surprisingly, Fletch lost that 1966 final.

SHIELDED FROM VICTORY

There seems to be one good reason why Queensland would secede from the rest of Australia—and it's got nothing to do with politics or mineral royalties. It's because of the elusive Sheffield Shield. More than a hundred years have passed since the Queensland Cricket Association was founded at 'the Gabba', and more than fifty since Queensland entered the Sheffield Shield competition. Yet not once in all that time has the state side triumphed.

Many local cynics strongly believe it's more than a question of cricketing ability. Even my mother used to talk about southern batsmen 'drawing the colour bar' and ensuring that Eddie Gilbert—the legendary Aboriginal bowler who was so fast he sent three southern batsmen to hospital in one innings—was sent back to his reserve. Then there was the time Victoria had the New South Wales team on its knees but didn't deliver the *coup de grace*—thereby stopping Queensland winning the shield.

At one stage the Queensland team contained Slasher Mackay, Peter Burge, Wally Grout and Ray Lindwall. But even with this combination they couldn't win—and there is much muttering into beers now about umpires in a certain state.

Thinking that maybe our players weren't good enough, Queensland a few years back bought Greg Chappell, the best batsman in the world, and Thommo, the best bowler, and test batsman Ian Davis, only to finish up second again—for the third year in a row.

Queensland bit the bullet and accepted that. But in 1977—the 100th anniversary of Queensland cricket and the 50th anniversary of shield participation—everything looked set at long last for a win. So Queensland built a new grandstand, hired a new curator to make fast wickets for Thommo and bought new covers to keep the rain out. There was some doubt by this time as to who was the best batsman in the world—Greg Chappell or Vivian Richards of the West Indies. So Queensland got them both.

By Christmas 1976 everything looked rosy and Queenslanders approached the New Year full of confidence and brotherly love. The end of the first half of the season saw Queensland a clear ten points in front and, though the team would be losing its stars for test cricket, so would the other states. The lead could be held.

But no. In January 1977 Queenslanders were aghast to find that Western Australia and South Australia somehow got to play an extra match while their test stars were still available—and, with a century by Marsh and ten wickets from Lillie, Western Australia leapt an insurmountable thirteen points past Queensland.

It would be difficult to imagine the feeling this created in Queensland; the gut feeling of being cheated of a dream. 'SHIELD DRAW RIGGED' cried the front page of the outraged Brisbane *Telegraph*. The Queensland Cricket Association executive committee chairman openly accused the Australian Cricket Board of 'tampering' with the shield draw to the detriment of Queensland.

After the W.A. match, Queensland could not, without its stars, make up the leeway. The state will never have a better team. It will never again have a better chance of winning the shield. And now this story will join all the other bitter stories passed down through successive Queensland generations.

THE MAROON AVENGERS

Fifteen Queenslanders wait locked in a grey brick room sitting with their backs to the walls. All are silent. All look only at the concrete floor. One is hunched up holding his stomach in a corner, as if he has been shot. He has not moved for thirty minutes.

Though all know me, none is to acknowledge my existence in the next ninety minutes in that crowded, bare room—not a wink, not a bump. In this room I feared I would be treated as an alien; instead I just do not exist.

For at this moment these fifteen men have the weight of the state of Queensland on their backs. They are, right now, the essence of the state—carefully distilled down through four generations of the Queensland private school system. They are also the product of four generations of losers, of Queenslanders succumbing to the superior numbers, better organization and greater finance of "the south".

Now, today—the day of the 1979 match—they are charged with wiping all those memories from the slate. This is why the fifteen are so uptight. Queensland teams have always found it impossible to win at sport—and many have lived for the day the cricket team, the league team or just any team would emerge national champions. Now, after two decades of planning, the state has produced this rugby team—a team of champions.

At least everyone hopes so.

Over and over again these young men have been told since school-days of the thrashings of old, right back to 1882 when New South Wales won the first game 28-4. And these fifteen know that in 1929 the New South Wales blues ran up a merciless 47 points—almost unheard of in top-grade rugby union—against the Queenslanders. That was fifty years ago today. And no one in the north is going to rest until that memory is eclipsed.

'Ninety to go,' says the manager John Ryan walking through the dressing room—and the ninety-minute run-up to the match begins. Queensland coach Bob Templeton signals that, for this fifteen at least, it has already begun. 'From now on we must have a single-mindedness of purpose,' he says.

Templeton doesn't rant or yell. This is far too serious for that. There is a Churchillian grimness about his speech, a desperate restraint which makes the listener lean forward. 'When you go back outside'—to warm up—'I want you to forget about girlfriends and relatives. Don't talk to anyone or think about them. You have only one purpose now'—and he leans forward across the wooden massage table—'to bloody well win.'

None of the fifteen looks up. Behind them on chrome pegs hang fifteen maroon jerseys in a line with new red socks carefully placed atop. The smallish bearded man in the corner, Andrew Slack, still sits wrapped around his stomach.

It was Slack who summed up the feelings for this match after training the previous Wednesday. A veteran of scores of representative matches against teams from all over the world, he inexplicably swung toward me and said: 'They don't waste much time coming around each year these New South Wales games.'

'Eighty minutes to go,' says John Ryan. Perhaps because he faces fifteen men sitting staring at the ground Templeton tells them to form two groups, backs and forwards, and go through again together what they must do. According to Ryan, team communication is one of the things behind this northern rugby revival. Team communication.

And while these fifteen go through this agony and gather reluctantly to talk when they have nothing to say, above their heads in the Murrayfield room of Queensland Rugby Union headquarters several hundred leading Queensland citizens talk furiously over food and drinks about the boys below. There is not the doubt here of the dressing room. The Queensland team has won the last four matches against New South Wales since 1975—the only time in history they have won four in a row. The previous week a New Zealand newspaper described this team as 'probably the strongest provincial-state-district rugby side in the world today'.

Confidence is so great here in the Murrayfield room that they talk not about the need to win today but—and everyone says the same thing over and over—'thrash them as they thrashed us for all those years'.

The room is filled with middle-aged lawyers, doctors, judges, newspaper executives, businessmen—the people who became the professionals two generations ago when the only schools were the GPS and other religious private schools. For Queensland is the only state where rugby union is played almost exclusively in GPS and private schools. Which means that the Queensland rugby team is always virtually a selection of the best old boys from twenty or so private schools—mainly GPS.

There is much talk about school representation here. It is a comment on Queensland rugby union that no one has to ask where any of the fifteen went to school—everyone knows. Quick mental arithmetic is done to decide whether 'Nudgee' or 'Terrace'—local jargon for the two Catholic GPS boys schools—has the greater representation. It is three-all.

A Nudgee old boy points out that giant forward and team captain Mark Loane and incomparable five-eighth Paul McLean are both Nudgee boys, in fact from the same Nudgee team. The lawyer opposite points out that Tony Shaw, who played against them at school for Terrace, is the Australian captain. Someone rattles off the results of the Nudgee and Terrace two-team school tours to New Zealand this year. Brisbane State High School, incongruously a GPS school by tradition, also has sent two teams to New Zealand. It is all part of today's winning plan.

In all, eight GPS or private religious schools are represented in the fifteen downstairs, and another three in the reserves. And these are the sort of statistics which show the way this 'old boy' group sticks together in business and in rugby—a sport which is now approached like a business.

'Forty-five to go,' says John Ryan and steps outside to explain that the business-like approach had its beginnings in 1962. For in that year

New South Wales announced that Queensland rugby was so poor that they would not play the annual match. And no wonder: in 1961 New South Wales won 29-0 and 45-0.

That's when the Queensland rugby types decided to do something about it. New president, Harry Edwards, a successful businessman, formed an under-nineteen competition to nurse the schoolboys along. And a Queensland team was sent to New Zealand—the first state overseas tour since 1893.

To overcome the problem of a borrowed ground with a small portable wooden stand four rows high, another president, solicitor Walter Boyd, in 1965 brought the considerable pressure of the rugby union men to bear and under the ALP Brisbane Lord Mayor, Alderman Clem Jones (an old GPS boy himself) obtained thirteen hectares of low-lying dump land just over a kilometre from the city centre. There they built Ballymore.

By 1976 they had the ground, the players—and they got Templeton to come back to coaching. They followed this up with twenty wins in succession against all comers at Ballymore before an ever growing crowd of admirers—a crowd whose rugby-following ranks are increasingly swelled with sport lovers from all other codes, out to see Queensland win. During the 1979 season the Queenslanders are expected to play before ninety thousand more spectators than four years ago.

In the dressing room the standard of that rugby administration was evident. Only eleven of the thirty players in the 1976 Queensland versus New South Wales clash are here today—ten in the Queensland team. They stopped players going to league or retiring by making them a team of friends so no one could really desert. When halfback Rod Hauser (St Peter's Lutheran College) retired this season and could not be replaced, the administration, the coach and the team went after him until he came back ... That was just a week ago.

'Twenty to go,' says Ryan, creating a flurry of activity now. This team want for nothing. A strapper is delegated to have plenty of laces, plaster, linament. A physiotherapist straps ankles. Zinc oxide plaster is wrapped around fingers, ankles, wrists—and backs and thighs rubbed with linament. Some are even putting vaseline on their boots. The two doors are shut and guarded from interruption.

Even Andrew Slack is out of his corner—briefly. He puts his number thirteen jersey on and, in contrast to all the others, that is his one preparation before retiring once more to his corner.

The strapper told me accurately where each would sit. 'You could come back in ten years and they would still be in those exact places,' he said. All except hooker Horton, who has been dropped to the reserves. No one has said anything to him, but he is not in his usual seat.

'Ten to go,' says Ryan and Paul McLean is still not dressed. He is dancing up and down and throwing his arms out in quick succession like a boxer, and alternately curling his fingers like a gunfighter.

McLean knows well he is the man on whom victory or defeat turns—yet he is the only relaxed figure in the room. He gives hope to rugby. For while players like him can succeed it will be an art rather than a contest. He is not big, not tall and doesn't look tough—in fact a stranger to the dressing room might pick him as a dancer. He has always been last strapped and last dressed, and last out. It is an unwritten law which none would dare to break.

The only other laws left now are on the field. And that is where the silence will be broken. At training this week Mark Loane told his forwards: 'As soon as you get into a contact situation let's hear that scream.'

'Drive, drive, drive ... rip, block,' they shouted as they foraged for the ball.

Even at training this match was uppermost in their minds. 'I knew who we were playing when I turned up for training Monday night,' said Paul McLean. 'The whole atmosphere had changed.'

Templeton concentrated at training on the backs sweeping like a ripple, and when a ball was dropped he said: 'Those bloody New South Wales blokes will get right up your arses.' They trained as if playing a match, and when Tony Shaw threw his clubmate Tony D'Arcy to the ground D'Arcy was carried off with a suspected broken ankle—and out of the reserves. Former Brisbane Grammar School first fifteen player and Queensland forward Alex Evans tells his fellow forwards as D'Arcy is carried off: 'This game on Sunday is the be all and end all. Let's think about it. We have to be ruthless with these ...'In the dressing room during training, green and orange signs read: 'Lineout: contest, dominate'; and 'Physical commitment'.

'Five to go,' says John Ryan. Fullback Bruce Cooke, a tall red head, who, like many in this team had a father who was a champion footballer—others include Duncan Hall and the McLean cousins—sits silently ready to go. He hasn't said anything in the four days I have watched this team.

Two over-anxious players start tossing a ball back and forth—and knock down a fluorescent light. 'Leave it. Leave it,' calls Templeton, and the semi-darkness adds a new dimension to the tension.

Andrew Slack looks the happiest he has been since he knocked off half a pavlova at the barbecue at former Queensland player, Dave Bedgood's place yesterday. The team gathered there to watch an ABC replay of New South Wales versus the Maoris. As the blues stood at attention for 'Advance Australia Fair', the Queenslanders broke up in laughter as someone said: 'That's the most composed they'll look this week.'

At the barbecue, Templeton told the story of how Bradman told his players at 3 for 400 to keep going 'because when you are on top you have to grind the opposition down to keep them down'. When the team heard their usual ankle strapper, physiotherapist Col O'Brien, was leaving the barbecue to catch a plane in an hour for an overseas conference, half of them lined up to have their ankles strapped then and there. No baths last night for them.

When Andrew Slack left the party (his ankles having been the first to be strapped), Loane commented that Slack and his flatmate, team breakaway Greg Cornelson, were going home to 'melancholy mansions'.

'Three to go,' says Ryan while Templeton bends over Slack whispering in his ear like a father-confessor. The strapper turns anxiously to me: 'This is the test match,' he says, instantly downgrading the internationals.

Templeton speaks to the whole team now, after his series of private talks with players: 'Shut everything else out. Only one thing matters now—success. What I am asking from you is physical commitment. You must give everything,' and he lingers on the last word.

There is nowhere for an outsider to hide in this emotion-charged room. Tony Shaw, his face masked with vaseline, is walking around shaking hands with his team as if he is never going to see them again.

'Two to go,' says Ryan.

'Paul,' says Templeton, and everyone stops. This is what they have been waiting to hear. Though they all know Paul McLean is untouchable as a five-eighth, southern critics refuse to acknowledge his unique talent. This morning it has been suggested he be put on the wing or at fullback in the Australian team. 'Why not play him breakaway or hooker,' says a team member at the news, 'and bat Greg Chappell number eleven,' says another. So strong is the feeling that one official advertisement billed the match as 'Paul McLean versus ...' and named seven southern rugby writers.

'Paul, we know you are the world's best five-eighth. Go out and prove it once and for all today,' says Templeton.

'One to go,' says Ryan.

Outside, the big crowd includes many who have never seen a union match before in their lives, and there is standing room only.

Loane, a bigger and faster version of a big, fast rugby forward, steps forward like the great Lord of Luna and breaks his ninety minutes' silence: 'This is it. Let's get up in the air ...' and I am ushered out to give them their last emotional seconds alone.

Their victory is history now: but not only did they win, they obliterated all the thrashings of the past—surpassing even the 47-point beating of 1929—by winning 48-10.

Queensland Rugby Union president, Joe Gibson, told the team's reception later: 'I want to say to New South Wales: Queensland has gone through this sort of a time. We tried to smile. We know how difficult it is. So we set about creating a team we could be proud of. I'm proud.'

And Mark Loane, the Nudgee boy who at eighteen became the

Queensland captain, had the last say. A man New Zealand papers have described as running downfield like a Melbourne Cup winner, a man who commands such respect at Ballymore that when he scores he is given a standing ovation all the way back to his own half, Loane said: 'We have received thrashings right back to the old days. They say it is character building.'

It certainly built a strong team of Queenslanders.

AN ENERGETIC FLUTTER AT EAGLE FARM

It is an understatement to say that at first sight Jim Kennedy, reputed to be Queensland's most flamboyant man of money, is a disappointment. As a man who has spent millions in recent years buying Queensland island tourist resorts he could at least have worn a brightly coloured, open-necked shirt ... and thongs. Instead, he contrasted with the entire Saturday population of Brisbane's Breakfast Creek Hotel as he stood at the bar in grey cabinet-minister type three-piece suit with narrow black stripes.

The recent seller of a million-dollar stud who brings in partners on his champion racehorses so he will have someone to celebrate the wins with, he might at least have spoken loudly, sworn, and used plenty of terminology like roughie, goer, and dud. Instead he spoke quietly and intensely.

A man who started with nothing and built up the biggest privately owned group of electrical stores in Australia (as far as anyone knows), who salvaged Japanese tuna boats wrecked on the Barrier Reef, who individually pulled off a multi-million-dollar takeover of a company on the stock exchange, and who recently escorted *Playboy*'s vivacious Playmate International to the races in the state where she is banned in photographic form, Jim Kennedy might have at least been large and aggressive. Instead he is a smallish man with short fair hair (greying now at the age of forty-four), glasses and schoolboyish face. Only the thin lips give any hint of the tough man inside. A million-dollar hit man, he might at least have been the son of a grazier or businessman. But his father was a schoolteacher.

In all, Jim Kennedy looked exactly what he is—an accountant, a product of a Brisbane GPS Catholic School (St Joseph's College, Nudgee) who left school after World War II but before Bill Haley and his Comets. Which makes him a bit like Burl Ives's Mr In-Between.

Unlike the older Australian business czars Kennedy did not inherit his start, nor did he strike out in a moment of enthusiasm and hit a one-up winner like many a younger tycoon. Rather, Kennedy did it all with a balance sheet—and, when chips were still fried potatoes, with a computer-like brain programmed to calculate immediately the smallest nuances of difference between two tables of figures.

So much, in fact, does Kennedy rely upon his brain to keep his private businesses ahead of their imposing opposition—like Ansett and TAA, the Queensland government's electricity department, every big company selling electrical goods—that he spends his Saturday off exercising his brain.

'I go to the races because you have to keep your wits about you and try to outsmart everyone. It is like mental exercise for the brain muscles,' is the way he put it.

The races would be an insight into the working of the man's mind and, anyway, a sojourn at Brisbane's premier racetrack with the evocative name of Eagle Farm promised to be a very nice way to spend a hot afternoon. I had visions of champagne in the air-conditioned bar, bundles of rolled up $50 bills, as we relaxed in the members' stand watching graceful horses canter past the mirrored finish post. No doubt there'd be a three-course lunch with heavy silver.

But again Jim Kennedy proved he was more businessman than showman. He rarely left the betting ring. With betting book in one hand and pen in the other he computed odds, mixed in the known character of various bookies and a dozen other variables and placed bets on the Sydney, Melbourne and Brisbane fields all at once. As a concession to my presence he did not bet on Southport because there would never have been any time for questions. As it was, Kennedy seemed keener that I should understand the gee-gees than that I should understand him: like a cricket fan taking an American to the Gabba.

'You watch for the southern shorteners,' he said as he disappeared to place a bet on a Brisbane race. He was gone before I could ask what he meant—but because he was the most conservatively dressed man in the members' enclosure I quickly found him again. What he wanted me to do—though he had already done it at a glance—was to watch the betting written on a blackboard next to the Sydney and Melbourne horses. If a horse's price was falling then he knew inside money was going on it late. At the same time you had to watch which local bookies were taking notice of this movement—'You have to imagine the mentality of the bookies,' he said. One horse was staying the same price, but a certain bookie was not giving such a good price. Kennedy found this significant.

'He is obviously scared of it, he is expecting money on it and he would know. The next call it will shorten to 7/2.' It did.

'You have to know the backbone of the bookies and how they operate. Some are opinion bookies and change as opinion changes—some are percentage bookies and ignore opinion.' Surprisingly, Kennedy talked with his competitors—the bookies—and exchanged opinions with them.

In many ways the ring resembled an ants' nest because almost everyone stopped opposite each other momentarily as they passed for a quick exchange of information—as ants invariably do. Since betting depends on odds I would have thought the thing to do would be to recommend what you weren't backing, but Kennedy invariably tipped what he was backing.

As he strode quickly around the ring—with its concrete floor and ugly yellow steel railings—Kennedy carried no money. He just whispered his bets to bookies, which was disappointing for one hoping to see lots of folding stuff. 'It is all on trust—racing is the most honest business in the world when it comes to taking thousands on trust,' he said. Then without warning: 'I would say they know a lot about this Rapid Romance. They would have to,' said Kennedy rushing off to make a winning bet on the basis that the bookies were scared of it (from the betting) and waiting for a plunge.

Kennedy backs a horse at 2-1 each way saying most punters would consider this was crazy but that statistics show such a horse rarely fails to run a place. 'A horse that deserves to be 2-1 must be pretty good. Horses of three and four to one rarely run a place, but 2-1 will rarely fail.' It does run third.

Kennedy's objective is to either win $2,000 or lose no more than $2,000 because of the law that a punter will bet until he loses. He is $600 up after two races, then loses and swears—but only mildly. 'I'm a bad loser, I hate to lose,' he says almost apologetically. Which is understandable, since he has so many carefully planned theories. He backs the favourite in a race because the next horse is four to one. 'Bookies aren't fools—everyone likes to think something can beat the favourite, but if he was any good he wouldn't be four to one he would be two to one.' He is right again.

There is a welter race and Kennedy believes that the best bets in welters are not the horses with light weights, but those with heavy weights. 'There is a minimum weight in welters and handicappers have a natural tendency not to give a horse too much weight. I win a lot on welters.' But he doesn't back the absolute top weight because he didn't think it was fit enough—it wins nevertheless.

He spots a field and a horse called Mr Magic: 'Years ago they won big money with that horse at Bundamba and now it is in Melbourne.' He backs it and it wins at seven to one.

A plea for lunch and we retire to a tiled room with a bar one side and hot food the other—and no tables or chairs in the wide space between. We stand there and eat two small pies each, with tomato sauce. Despite the hectic pace we manage the occasional drink, but I never finish a drink (or the pies) before Kennedy is off. 'I will meet you at the betting ring.' A few years ago he used to bring his secretary to help him keep up with the information.

My tired legs appreciate the three races we watch from the grandstand. 'I come to the races to bet and win money,' Kennedy says to my complaining that it wasn't the lazy afternoon I had expected.

He comments that owners of winners have nowhere to celebrate with their connections and the owners of the placed horses after a race. 'I have won classics here and gone to the bar by myself.' He points out the lack of colour at the Brisbane races (and the lack of youth) and says the organizers have forgotten that racing started with the 'I bet my horse can beat your horse' challenge. He indicates the huge area of wasted real estate in the middle of the track. We look at the paddock, which is supposed to be the classy area for non-members, and I note that the bar front is made up of yellow rolling garage doors. Kennedy wonders why the betting and the bar should be behind the grandstand away from the racing. He goes outside for a drink with top jockey Mick Dittman and laments that jockeys cannot enter the members' enclosure. 'If I ran my resorts like this ...' He shrugs.

He is up $1,400 and has reached the best late bet where he makes his plunge to win $2,000 for the day or nothing. He puts $1,000 on at 10/9 on—and it loses by a head. Kennedy doesn't like it, but this is not a big bet for him. Once he put $35,000 for a win on one of his horses. 'If you have your horse ready to win you have to have enough guts to back it for what it owes you,' he says with that same intensity with which he approaches life. 'If it cost you $15,000 and starts at two to one on you have to put $30,000 on it. It is not much fun but I have done it. You have to have a systematic approach.'

Then, just as quickly as he placed his bets, Kennedy is gone. He is not the type to hang about. Which probably explains how he went from selling stoves to running tourist islands and horse studs.

From school Kennedy entered his uncle's accounting firm and studied accountancy at night. He was so keen to do well that he would lock himself in a schoolroom at his father's school on weekends and throw the key out the window to his sisters, telling them not to let him out until 5 p.m.

'I guess I was a bright boy, I won lots of awards,' he said, recalling that the exams were Australia-wide in those days and that he topped the final year.

Before he was twenty-one he qualified and his second employer called him in and offered him ten shillings a day extra on top of his thirteen pounds a week. Kennedy said he was leaving, and showed what sort of businessman he was soon to become.

'You wouldn't walk out, Jim?' his employer said.

'I'm leaving now,' said the brash Kennedy.

He saw an accountant's job advertised at thirty pounds a week and applied. He thought he might look too young so—always covering possibilities—went out and bought a hat to look more the accountant. He got the job with an electrical firm and within a short time was manager. 'I always do things bang, bang,' said Kennedy, 'and I asked for a partnership.' The owner said he would have a talk to his wife and Kennedy replied: 'I don't want a partnership with a guy who has to talk to his wife about it first.'

At that stage Kennedy's biggest asset was a car on hire purchase. It was 1958 and he was twenty-three. He took some of the staff with him and decided to go into an electrical store himself. Typically, he went straight into the main street of Brisbane, 420 Queen Street, replacing an old wine saloon. 'We did it the hard way and went in cold,' he said. His father retired from teaching and joined him and Kennedy gave up accounting and started selling and working seven days a week.

A few years later, in 1961, the Menzies credit squeeze hit and electrical stores were among the first to suffer the withdrawal of the consumer. Kennedy, the calculator, still did well and he started buying other stores as they went broke. He kept some stores and with others just went for the stock.

'As things got rolling I got back into accounting and I was not against closing a store if it didn't do well. We were flexible and fluid and each store had to make a profit in its own right. Some closed because of things beyond our control. At Newstead the bureaucrats, who do what they want, put a dirty big bit of concrete in the middle of the road with the single-minded approach that they know what is good for everyone. You would think you would have the right to sue them, but we don't fight anymore, we just close them down, and we closed that store because no one could turn there anymore.'

Kennedy now has a dozen stores in Brisbane. He came through the credit squeeze of the sixties well off because he was 'harder, tougher and better'.

'You can't have high fixed overheads. I won't go into a shop with high rents, we are discounters and we can't afford that.' He is not impressed by the huge new airconditioned shopping complexes being built all over the place around Australia in the last few years.

'I have grave doubts about the validity of these centres—they are doing it at high cost and are replacing the quite adequate stores that are already there. The rents are so high I can't afford them and they are thus adding to inflation and pushing up prices.'

Kennedy runs his stores with the balance sheet precision of an accountant—there are objectives for just about everyone in the organization. 'Every day at 10 a.m. I get the complete story of yesterday—who did what and who didn't do what. And we know precisely what stocks we have—that's one area people get out of control.'

While he has incentive bonuses for staff, the sales staff know their jobs are on the line if they don't reach targets. 'All we are interested in is performance,' Kennedy says. 'There are a lot of nice people who can't sell. They should work somewhere else like the public service, we can't afford them.'

As his stores boomed Kennedy moved into all sorts of projects—he tried hair dressing shops, fruit shops, and ship salvaging, among others. The ship salvaging expedition however was such a disaster that Kennedy could manage only a thin grin when asked how much he lost. 'I wouldn't like to say. I told you, I'm a bad loser.' He and an American salvaged a 350-tonne Japanese tuna fishing boat off the Great Barrier Reef and had it refitted in Ballina and sent it hunting prawns in the Gulf of Carpentaria. They did another and sold it—but the cost of lifting the deck height for Europeans, among other things, made it a bad deal.

But Kennedy did not return chastened to the washing machine stand. He saw himself not as the owner of a chain of stores but as a professional businessman. 'Chartered accountants are well placed to be objective.' He looked at Bryces transport company, the shares of which were selling at about four dollars a share. Kennedy made his first headlines by pouring in a million dollars to take over the company and then sold off the assets. Admirers say he made a million or more in this hit, detractors say only a half million. He says it was 'a very good deal'.

'The opportunity for an individual to do this doesn't exist

anymore,' he lamented. 'The big merchant bankers are watching it all the time.'

The next year he diversified again—this time surprising everyone by buying an island resort—Tangalooma on Moreton Island, off Brisbane. A pilot himself with his own Italian Twin in those days, Kennedy built up Tangalooma air taxis to three planes and turned the resort from a quarter of a million turnover a year to one and a half million when he sold it in 1977.

In 1973, then aged thirty-nine, Kennedy was made a director of the Commonwealth Bank (the youngest by far) and the same year the federal Labor government appointed him to a Royal Commission into the Post Office which split it into Telecom and Australia Post. Then for two years he was made chairman of the Postal Commission to get it working.

After that he planned a break, but Alfred Grant's bankrupt company properties went up for auction and Jim Kennedy extended his horse racing interests beyond owning winners to owning a stud. He bought Wellcamp Stud near Toowoomba, built a racetrack, grew crops, filled it with horses, and restored the old homestead. But studs need customers and Wellcamp didn't have any. So Kennedy bought a stallion that had a chance of a win in the big winter carnival in Brisbane—Blue's Finito—and syndicated it immediately. It was oversubscribed the first morning. The horse won three big ones within three weeks, including the traditional big one, the Doomben Ten Thousand (now named after a cigarette brand and jacked up to a hundred thousand). Not only did the syndicate get its money back immediately but Kennedy suddenly had a full book of fifty top quality mares for his new stallion at Wellcamp, and it became one of the busiest studs in Australia.

In 1977 he found out that the traditionally popular Great Barrier Reef island resort of South Molle was up for grabs, and needed revitalizing. Kennedy bought it. Then he sold out of the Wellcamp stud in a million-dollar deal, but still owns about a hundred brood mares and has ten horses currently racing. About half of these he leases with his friends—to have someone to celebrate with.

As a general practitioner in the world of business tycoons Kennedy doesn't fear fellow businessmen—but gets very upset at competing against government bodies with taxpayers' funds behind them.

'I resent governments in business. They have no right there,' he says. His electrical stores are up against the state government electricity distributor which runs its own stores. 'Anyone who deals with these stores needs to have their head read—the state can't even supply electricity half the time,' he said, forgetting his accountant's background. His South Molle resort is up against, as he says, the federal government in the form of TAA. 'We don't mind being up against Ansett with their Hayman but TAA run Dunk and Keppel Islands. Wherever I look I see government unwarrantedly in business.' He said TAA was in a position to direct passengers to their resorts instead of to private ones—and TAA should have to disclose separately the books of these businesses as they were funded with community money.

'I have grave doubts that they are making money,' he said.

Kennedy believes the two airline system has had its day and believes that if the Queensland tourist industry is to do any good 'we have got to do a Honolulu and go it along'.

'Queensland has got to promote Queensland in its own right internationally or all the tourists will end up in the Hiltons of Sydney and Melbourne. It's the trap for young players. I wouldn't discount the thought of Queensland getting its own airline—it's wide open. I do have grave doubts about what the federal government and international airlines do for us. Just look at our airport compared to the others.'

Kennedy didn't say anything about it, but I know he has privately talked of hiring his own Boeing jet and pilots, loading it up in Sydney and taking off for north Queensland. If he decides to do it he will. Not long ago he opened all his stores at night in defiance of government rules, issued press statements, ignored inspectors, and the ten-year battle for night shopping in Queensland was won in a few weeks.

Kennedy also dislikes the way the press tends to write successful businessmen up as 'lucky playboys'—'I have worked my guts out and, while I may appear to be a lucky playboy, I'm not,' he said.

Which turned out to be half true. At the races he drank soda water. But there was a good reason: 'Last night I ran into these two mates of mine and we have this long standing thing that when we see each other one of us buys a bottle of champagne, and then the other and, of course the other and ...'

THE BUSH CAN BE A BASTARD

TRUE GRIT

Pat Moran is so tough that for many years he washed his hair with Solvol soap. His fingers are so big and so hardened that when his daughter found a deadly red-back spider on a biscuit tin in the corrugated iron shed that is his home, he walked over and crushed it with his forefinger. Pat continued our conversation as if he had just stubbed out a cigarette. It was the same when he killed the black scorpion on the concrete floor of the shed, and the two snakes the next morning while still bare-footed—all done matter-of-factly, and without comment.

Pat Moran is not an average suburban Australian. After spending a decade fighting nature for the right to twelve thousand acres of northern Australia—in an area known in Queensland as 'the brigalow'—Pat, at thirty, has the lean body of a teenage surfie, and the out-of-proportion forearms of a Sumo wrestler. Burnt a red tan they hang, Popeye-like, below his slender shoulders. He has that other characteristic of the Australian grazier: swollen fingers, puffed up and marked by too many fights with barbed wire fences, tractor nuts, splintered fence posts and rearing horses. If Pat Moran were ever to play a piano or use a typewriter, the keys would have to be set twice as wide apart.

He has a bony lump on his right shoulder, one on his right wrist, and one on his back—the legacy of injuries he left too late to be treated. Recently when a cow gored him through his shoe while he was mustering on horseback he did not want to go to the doctor but his wife, Geraldine, talked him into it and he had eleven stitches in the wound.

Not that he, or others like him, would see this as all that tough. But when your living depends on taming bulls, stallions, and trees it is obvious that only the physically tough and tenacious will stay.

During the slump many graziers didn't muster the cattle that were hard to get and now these have gone wild, like feral pigs. They call them 'scrubbers' because they run for the scrub when chased on horseback, and are hard to catch. A few years ago these cattle were worth almost nothing, now they are worth three to four hundred dollars and many cattlemen are building traps around waterholes to get them. Recently Pat managed to round up several 'Mickey' bulls (uncastrated wild cattle) but he says they are too hard to get without traps.

'They head for the river country where there are big holes in the ground and you try to follow at a gallop and you land ten yards in front of your horse. By the time you get up and get your horse he is gone.'

Some of these cattle are too shrewd even to trap at waterholes—Pat says they won't even come out of the scrub for water, they stay in there and eat the juice from prickly pear.

Geraldine mentions that I am lucky I just missed the sandflies—Pat says they were so bad down near the river that the kangaroos were groggy, one of the stallions came into the shed to try to escape them and Pat himself had to tie a handkerchief around his face like a bandit so he didn't breathe them in.

Life in the bush, of course, has always been tough, but what made it so much tougher was a complete lack of money during the five-year cattle slump.

The heat in the daytime in the big tin shed is unbearable. It has no internal walls—a row of three clothes cupboards and a kitchen cupboard separates the beds from the living area. There is no TV, no stereo, no carpet, no paintings of beach scenes on the walls, no dishwasher, no en suite, no shades on the lights. The backseat of a car forms part of the monastic lounge and the cupboards are not old enough to be solid timber and not modern enough to be veneered. The stove is fired by wood. It is almost as if Myers and Japan have been deliberately excluded from their lives.

To keep some money coming in during the slump, Geraldine, a blonde with the looks of a *Vogue* model, worked in a garage dining room, then as a teacher's aide and, more recently, cleaning the school. This meant that Pat had to go mustering through the brigalow with his daughter Chelsea, then aged one, sitting on the saddle in front of him and his son, Kane, then three, hanging on from behind. Which slowed him down a little.

Now, while Kane is at school, Geraldine goes mustering with little Chelsea, four, sitting on the horse's rump and holding on to mum's jeans with both hands and bouncing up and down as they canter through the bushes. When the going gets too rough, or Geraldine has to gallop through scrub, she sets Chelsea down one-handed on the nearest log and returns for her later.

It is a real family affair—but then that was the whole idea of the idealistic Brigalow Scheme which was started to put ordinary country people onto their own cattle properties. The Queensland government borrowed federal money and poured $20 million into a scheme to open up one and a half million hectares of undeveloped brigalow land in central Queensland. It was divided into 250 blocks of varying size, depending on the quality of the land. The idea was that each block should be big enough when developed to hold about 2,000 head of cattle, and thus provide the family with a good income after the initial development period.

The government knew that this country would be difficult to develop because it is very hard to stop brigalow regrowth which kills the grass. Also it would be expensive. So a scheme was arranged which, it was hoped, would attract people keen enough to beat the tree regrowth problem on this land, and supply them with the finance to do it. People like Pat. Unfortunately no one realized a big cattle slump was just around the corner.

Pat Moran started entering ballots for a brigalow selection, as they are officially called, when he was seventeen, and four years later his name came up. He went before a selection tribunal and filled the requirements—he was aged between eighteen and fifty-five, he was a man (women can not apply), 'physically capable', he had assets of $10,000 and the asset backing of "a close relative" for $26,000. Pat had also been working for more than three years as a grazier—since leaving school he had worked on his father's cattle property in western Queensland, and took almost all of his wages in cattle. His asset backing therefore was in the form of a small herd of cows.

The brigalow block he drew was halfway between Rockhampton and Mackay—in tropical Australia. The government listed $34,000 worth of improvements including about three thousand acres of cleared brigalow, and put the purchase price at $32,000. Under the scheme, the purchase price is not payable immediately—but over twenty-five years in interest-free instalments. Because of the big expense in developing such blocks—and the lack of capital of the applicants—up to $72,000 a block is available in low interest loans to build yards, dams, buy cattle, clear trees, build fences, sheds, and sow improved grasses. In a rather optimistic view of what might be done, applicants were given five years 'to destroy timber growth and sow improved grasses and maintain the property free of suckers'.

Pat faced some pretty strict requirements. In the first year he had to build a cattle dip and yards, by the second the entire property had to be enclosed with a substantial fence and the third year had to see sufficient subdivisional fencing and dams 'for the efficient working of the property'. He had to live on the property for at least seven years. Once all this had been done, and all debts repaid, he would own the business.

Optimistically Pat set off from his father's property near Boggabilla with 'a heap of dogs' and drove his cattle north to Miles, before putting them on trucks.

It was 1971 and cattle prices were good. Pat paid to have two and a half thousand acres of land cleared of brigalow, built the boundary fences and bought an old bulldozer to put in dams. Using steel tramlines he built a stout dip and holding yard with concrete base and started on internal fencing. He had a big shed built, as all of the brigalow people did as a temporary home for a few years until a homestead could be built—when the shed would be used to store hay.

Then, in 1973, the cattle crash came with Japan cancelling all beef orders and the U.S. cutting back—and almost all the brigalow people, including Pat, were left stranded in their tin sheds. With cattle worth only one-fifth of the expected price, incomes were too low to afford property improvements. So just to keep going, Pat built roads with his dozer for a living, broke horses, and helped build other people's fences.

Meanwhile, the dreaded brigalow scrub quickly regained hold as the new suckers grew out of the old roots. As these grew the improved grasses died—and cattle that hid in them were difficult, if not impossible, to muster. Cattle learned to crawl through cheaply built fences. Pat could not afford the grass to burn paddocks—which helps destroy the suckers, helps control ticks, worms and grasshoppers, and keeps the grass sweet for the cattle.

People like Pat could not buy the good bulls they needed to stop inbreeding, so they bought cheap bulls—'which goes dead against my grain,' said Pat in his only outburst. 'That's your downfall. One bad bull and you can't breed him out again for ten years unless you have such big numbers you can afford to cull out all the cows by him.' Bad bulls, Pat said, breed smaller cattle that take longer to grow.

Geraldine said it was extremely frustrating working for five years and making no money and watching the property go backwards and the suckers get higher and higher. The only thing that saved them and thousands of other cattlemen was plenty of rain. A drought would have seen them all broke.

'I was starting to think that when you draw one of these brigalow blocks you have to win the Golden Casket lottery with it,' Pat said.

By 1978 Pat was more than $20,000 behind in repayments—though the department had suspended payments for two years—and $6,000 in arrears for rates. Monetarily he was less in debt than many because Pat had allowed other graziers to put cattle on his land in return for money to help him survive. But this meant that when the recovery began he was only half stocked.

The prices recovery in 1979, though, had a dramatic effect on his situation. Now, when Pat sends a semi load of cattle—twenty cows or fat bullocks—to market he gets $5,000 instead of $1,000. He planned to pay back half of his $20,000 debt with just two semi loads.

Which is fine—while it lasts. But the boom is not expected to continue for long, and then men like Pat Moran will have to tough it out once again.

THE GOOD OIL

Charlie Jones, the only man in Australia who personally owns an oil refinery, just can't help doing things differently. While everyone else in the western Queensland town of Roma seems to drive around in a Holden utility, Charlie Jones, even in his fifties, prefers a decade-old white E-type Jaguar. And, while the rest of the population in those parts favour wide-brimmed felt hats, Charlie Jones covers the grey bristles of a near-crewcut with a silver hard hat.

Instead of a homestead he lives in a rented flat, and when he drives out of town to work each day on his property among the wheatfields he has no tractors or horses, no ploughs or cattle. Charlie Jones works inside a portable building full of dials and automatic graphs. Outside, the property looks like an old, abandoned service station site that once went to absurd lengths to attract passing motorists by building a scaled-down model of a moon rocket station—and failed.

This is Charlie's refinery—the smallest in Australia, the only inland oil refinery in Australia, the only one built by an individual, the only one made from second-hand parts, the only refinery owned by a man and his family. It is also unique in a much more important way, the way petrol prices are going. It is the only refinery which holds out hope for Australia to use up its inland oil pools which are starting to prove too small and too far away to make pipelines viable. It will also save people in these remote areas from having to rely on fuel for their cars and machinery being transported all the way from the coast.

That's why Charlie Jones built 'the darn thing'. It started producing three years ago and now refines thousands of gallons of petrol a day, as well as distillate for farm machinery, trucks and such like, and more than enough fuel oil to supply the local abattoir. The refinery now supplies four different service stations in Roma (population 6,500) with petrol—Ampol, Caltex, Esso and BP—plus service stations up to two hundred kilometres away in Charleville and Dirranbandi. And when strikes or breakdowns have caused coastal shortages, Charlie Jones has shipped his products as far as Brisbane and even over the border into New South Wales.

In all he feeds 400 barrels of crude or gas condensate a day into his mini-refinery from up to seven tiny fields near Roma. And every gallon he produces in Roma saves bringing it by tanker all the way from the coast.

Charlie Jones, a tallish, lean Texan, came to Australia in 1968 as one of the many overseas experts brought in during the mining boom. His job was to supervise drilling and production, a job which had already taken him around the globe. In all, he supervised the drilling of seventeen holes in Australia—and five were gas producers, mainly in the Roma area. Then, in 1971, the company he was working for collapsed with Minsec and Charlie Jones was out of a job. But he had noted in his drilling days that there was enough crude and gas condensate in the Roma area to operate a small refinery—and enough people in the area to buy what was produced. He did his mathematics and saw that he could build a small refinery and, as he put it, make money.

In those days the government-fixed price for crude oil was $2.15 a barrel. It was costing Roma area producers 75 cents per barrel to truck it 250 kilometres to Moonie, plus 53 cents per barrel pipeline tariff to send it to Brisbane. So, Charlie Jones worked out, the producers were getting only about 87 cents per barrel at the well head. By sending their production to a local refinery, the producers could cut their trucking costs and eliminate the pipeline tariff. Jones worked out that he could split the savings with producers so they would be ahead and he would get cheaper crude oil and gas condensate. Everybody would be happy.

So Charlie Jones, who was familiar with small privately owned refineries in the U.S. and other countries, decided to give it a go.

'I suppose until you get it built no one can believe one person can build a refinery. It's a bit like going in to ask for a loan to build a spaceship to the moon.'

Then Charlie tried all the oil refineries and, in the end, the Queensland Department of Industrial Development agreed to back him for half the money. Ampol decided it would come in with the other half.

The project could be a prototype for the future in Australia. Charlie Jones reasoned that if the refinery worked at Roma one could be built near any future inland oil discoveries where the reserves might be too small to warrant construction of a pipeline to the coast, but where there were enough people to use the products. There were already some other inland areas in this situation, he said. Alice Springs had nearby oil which could supply the town with petrol in the future. Winton in western Queensland, and northwest Western Australia were other possible places.

There were other places though where a refinery like this would not be desirable. The Cooper Basin in South Australia had enough gas condensate liquids to produce 15,000 barrels a day of petrol but only a dozen or so consumers within a hundred kilometres. 'There you have to have a pipeline,' he said.

His decision made, Jones went to the U.S. and for $5,000 bought a copy of a design for a small refinery drawn up for the Persian Gulf. Then he went searching for suitable equipment. From a shut down coal tar distillation unit at Mortlake in Sydney—'a fairly exotic plant that was no longer in operation"—he bought second-hand pumps, heat exchangers, vessels and valves. A petrochemical plant at Silverwater in New South Wales was being demolished, so Charlie Jones moved in for two heaters, a gas compressor and a vessel. Then from Total's Matraville refinery in Sydney he bought two reactors and two heat exchangers and trucked them all up to western Queensland.

Then, of course, he had to put it all together. And it works, although Charlie Jones has been innovative, to say the least: the machine for measuring vapour pressure sits in holes cut in an old Hoovermatic washing machine which agitates the water bath. 'We got it cheap at ten dollars,' he said.

By 1976 the plant was operationable, but he ran into many technical problems which took some time to iron out. Now, he says, his problems are mostly economic, because the cost of crude has changed so much (as a result of government policy) since the original refinery was designed.

Although his refinery is an effective means of using Australia's small inland pools of oil, it does not mean he can do it cheaper. Certainly the cost of transporting crude oil to the coastal refineries and then sending the refined products back to Roma is saved, but the small inland refinery cannot operate as economically as the larger refineries.

The Charlie Jones refinery breaks a barrel of crude down to about 37 per cent naphtha, 30 per cent distillate and 26 per cent fuel oil. The naphtha is a low octane raw petrol that is not suitable for use in today's automobiles—though it would run a T-model Ford. To raise the octane the naphtha is put through a catalytic reformer and then put into a stabilizer to provide petrol volatility to suit expected local temperatures. In the process of conversion to finished products about 10 to 12 per cent of each barrel is lost as gases, which Jones burns for fuel to run the four refinery heaters.

He is lucky that there is a local market for the heavy fuel oil in the abattoir, otherwise it would be difficult to sell locally. Part of the fuel oil could be 'cracked' to increase the refinery yield of petrol and distillate, but this would increase the cost of the refinery and the complexity of operation—and would still leave a large amount of excess fuel oil.

Another thing which keeps the price of fuel from his small refinery up is staff. He employs eight operators and two supervisors, and they put through about forty barrels a man a day. Refineries operating on a larger scale can put through four hundred or more barrels a man. However he says he can double capacity in the future without putting more men on. Charlie Jones also has to produce the products the local market will buy. For example, he could easily produce kerosene, but he could not sell it locally.

To try to explain the problems caused by new government oil pricing policies Charlie Jones wrote a submission to the government. He pointed out that he faced a high risk factor since he was dependent on the one oil field, and any oil field was subject to the possibility of a sharp production decline which would make his refinery uneconomic. He also argued that the prices he could charge were set by the prices of equivalent products produced at the nearest coastal refinery—plus the freight cost. He therefore had no say in pricing.

Charlie Jones felt he should be able to buy the crude cheaper than the government-set figure which the coastal refineries pay because he is on-the-spot. And he feels that he too should be paid the freight subsidy because of the disadvantages of operating a refinery so far inland. For the freight subsidy lowers costs for his coastal competition.

Since future on-land oil discoveries in Australia are likely to be relatively small and probably remote, his project could be very important to Australia. He points out that at present there 'are fewer than a dozen' drilling rigs operating in Australia while in the U.S., a country of similar area and where oil drilling has been going on since early this century, there are (he checks a journal) 2,152 rigs running. In Canada there are 353 listed. 'They are drilling a lot of dry holes, but they are also finding new reserves of oil,' he said.

Although many people were pessimistic about finding oil in great quantity in inland Australia, the world crude oil situation was such that Australia had to find out. 'And the only way you can find out if it's there is to drill holes.'

And Charlie Jones knows the search can be a heartbreaking gamble: in the late 1950s he poured twenty years of savings into five dry holes in the U.S. 'But I could have made a million.'

THE BIG GUNN OUT OF ACTION

Sir William Gunn, the last of the big, big men from those halcyon days of Menzies and McEwan when Australia really did ride on the sheep's back, sprawled lower and lower across the settee as he spoke of the impossibilities of developing Australia's top end.

'I should have realized what was ahead when I first went there to clean up the Humpy Do American rice project and saw thousands of geese eat all the rice,' he told me as he cast his mind back to the early 1950s when Australia thought it had all the answers.

Sir William, now in his mid-sixties, still sports the short-back-and-sides hair-parted-down-the-middle style of the 1949 Wallaby tourists. But when I spoke to him in March 1977 his hair was ruffled and, though men from Queensland's Goondiwindi district are not supposed to cry, there was moisture around his eyes as he said: 'I'm sad, and I'm embarrassed, wouldn't you be?'

Normally Sir William is described as having the physique and face of a heavyweight boxer, but he looked to me more like a beast brought to its knees by the abattoir sledgehammer. The week before, five of his pastoral companies had gone into receivership.

Big Bill Gunn first took on the Territory when a group of Americans asked him to go to Humpy Do and see what was wrong with their rice project. 'I said to them "What the hell do I know about rice?" I knew nothing about rice then and I still don't. But I could see when I got there that it was one hell of a mess. The manager had employed a whole lot of blacks to shoot the wild geese who were eating the rice. With any agricultural pursuit there is always a problem with birds but what had happened there was that they had failed to plough properly and the weeds that grow so fast there had taken over. So the only way they could get the rice in was to drop it from an aeroplane into the weeds, and the geese were coming and just picking it up. That's a true story. One of the Americans had spent two hundred thousand dollars on planting—two hundred thousand to feed geese from aeroplanes.'

Sir William said he dismissed all the staff and closed the rice project down. 'After sacking everyone I went to America and refinanced the place and got out. They insisted on refinancing and one man put in a million pounds and two years later they got me to go and have another look and I told him he had done his dough.' Sir William said that this time there was a beautiful crop of rice but the harvesters had not arrived at the property. 'They of course had another lawyer in charge and I went in as the unofficial liquidator and sold any assets and paid the creditors money they would never have got otherwise.'

Others tell a different version—and blame Gunn for heading a rice project in the Territory that went bust.

'Yes I know history records me differently. But that's what happened. I wouldn't have anything to do with the rice, I went in as unofficial liquidator. It has been said I was responsible for feeding the ducks but that was how it was when I found it.'

Though Sir William was Australia's Mr Big of wool and meat and spent his time travelling from company board-rooms to meetings with cabinet ministers, like so many others he caught the Top End bug.

'I reckoned it had potential,' he told me.

In the late 1950s a Singapore group of Chinese and Englishmen took out an option to purchase the two-and-a-half million acre Tipperary property in the Territory and they asked Sir William to look after it for them 'because they didn't know anything about cattle'.

'I recognized the tremendous potential then,' he said. 'In the first five years I might say we made money. But while the Singapore group had put up the original capital they had not put up enough to develop the potential.

'There was another American group looking for land in the Territory and I put them into Cape York—but that's another story. The Americans bought Tipperary. I had sold it to them on the basis of a cattle property. Then I started receiving cables telling me to grow grain. I told them it was a hell of a risk up there and they said to plant ten thousand acres in the first year.' Sir William said CSIRO advice was not to try it. 'But they said they had plenty of money and could afford the risk. They said that if it was a complete failure they would just do it again.'

In August he planted thirteen thousand acres. Then Gunn and the Americans disagreed over the next step. Because of the big wet in the Territory he said they must buy huge dryers—the Americans said they were unnecessary. The Americans told him to buy molasses from Queensland to feed the cattle, but he argued that the cost of getting it would be prohibitive. 'I refused to buy the molasses and they wouldn't buy the dryers. Then they wanted to feed the sorghum stubble to breed calves in a feedlot, that's a true story, and of course the calves died in the feedlot. Then in the middle of the big wet—you know what the wet's like in the Territory—they told me to do things while the place was about ten feet under water. Anyway by March we had the best crop of sorghum grown in the Territory—including in research—and a week later I walked out.'

And all the while Sir William Gunn—despite the geese problems and the difficulties with calves dying in the feedlot—was becoming one of the most influential men in Australia. He became chairman of the Australian Wool Board (a position he held for a decade) in 1963 and that year, when he proposed doubling the woolgrowers' levy to pay for development of new markets, he was pelted with eggs and fruit at a public meeting in the Victorian town of Hamilton. He advocated a reserve price for wool which was rejected by growers' referendums in 1951 and 1965 but introduced in 1970 as an emergency measure to save the industry.

A fourth generation son of a Goondiwindi grazing family, Gunn became a member of the Commonwealth Bank Board for five years, sat on the Export Development Council between 1962 and 1965, and has been a director of the Reserve Bank of Australia since 1959. He was a member of the Australian Meat Board for thirteen years and by 1965 he was considered the probable future leader of the Country Party in Australia. The federal leader of the party, Jack McEwan, backed Sir William for preselection for the safe Country Party seat of Maranoa in Queensland. McEwan had lost the older party stalwarts like Sir Arthur Fadden and Sir Earle Page and wanted Sir William as his successor. But Gunn had many critics in the electorate and they rejected him at the pre-selection for a then relatively unknown candidate.

Sir William said that, after his other experiences, he felt he knew the Territory, and his family bought a half-million-acre property there called Douglas. 'We used the income from Goondiwindi to develop Douglas steadily and we didn't borrow any money. By 1969 we knew most of the answers of what to do and decided to borrow and we bought our American partner out—and that's where I went wrong. You can't borrow money and survive in the north of Australia. Everything is too big and too costly. Once you borrow money in the Territory you are headed for receivership.'

Sir William said the difficulties of the Territory were magnified by the fact that there were several small meatworks instead of one big one in Darwin which should have been government subsidized to allow cattlemen to get on their feet. 'They all wanted their own meatworks and now they are closing them down. If you can't put fifty thousand head a year through a meatworks the producer is subsidizing it. The meatworks in the Territory can only pay low prices because of the high cost of operating their low through-put. And one big meatworks at Darwin would have meant cheaper transport—it's cheaper to move cattle than meat.' Sir William said all the cattle along the northern part of Australia across to Queensland's Gulf country should be taken to Darwin for slaughtering.

'The Territory should have been a great place to invest. You had the cheapest land in Australia and cheap labour in the form of Aboriginals who were happier then than they are today because the stations looked after them. They were gainfully employed but now the do-gooders have made them unhappy.'

Sir William said his station cattle did well but by the time the operation really got going in 1973 the bottom had fallen out of the cattle market. The real problem for Gunn was that this collapse in prices also affected his Goondiwindi properties which had been subsidizing Douglas and paying off the high interest payments. 'If we hadn't bought the American partner out we could have managed all right. But Douglas dragged us down and took the family properties with it,' he said.

Sir William, understandably, is not optimistic about the rural future of Australia. 'Once it was a way of life, not a business to pay the necessary return on capital invested. But it is no longer a way of life, it is too tough. Husbands only manage now throughout Queensland and the Territory because their wives have become their offsiders. My two daughters are in that position so I know. I defy you to go and find a house painted on these properties in the last four years.'

So Sir William Gunn, one of Australia's best known rural power figures for thirty years, became just another scalp on the belt of Australia's north. The giant Ord River Scheme in Western Australia found the going too tough. The ambitious Lakeland Downs cattle property on Cape York couldn't make it despite the backing of Queensland millionaire Clive Foyster. And then Sir William Gunn, the Queenslander whose judgment was respected by many, bogged down in the dust and heat of the Top End.

BULLDUST AND BOREWATER

The face of Chris Herrmann, the boss drover, is a Central Australian red, even though he wears his broad-brimmed digger's hat so much that he looks strange without it on—like a bearded man who has suddenly shaved. In the bar and sometimes in bed in his swag ('to keep the moonlight out') Chris Herrmann's pale blue eyes peer out from under his shadowy hat. His boots are size eleven, and he rolls his own from a blue tin of Capstan in white Tally-ho papers. He's in his fifties but his stomach goes in rather than out. If you said he was wiry, the analogy would have to be with barbed wire.

Because of the immense danger of bushfires in the foot-deep dry grass stretching in all directions as far as the eye can see, he stubs out his cigarettes in the palm of his left hand, after giving it a lick.

The only place Chris Herrmann bulges is in the forearms, where muscles stand up like ropes and work seemingly independent of the body. But he would never win a gun battle in a cowboy film—his giant fingers just wouldn't fit through the trigger guard of a Colt .45. Chris Herrmann carries his belongings in a steel .303 cartridge box. But rather than overflowing with cans of beer it is filled with round tins of tobacco for the droving trip. There are no double-breasted suits in the West and Chris Herrmann wears long, tight blue jeans that make the circle of his tobacco tin stand out below the leather pouch that houses his pocket knife.

Never far from his favoured left hand are his stockwhip and his long white lasso. The pocket of his khaki shirt (rolled to the elbows) holds the green diary which contains the little maps he has drawn on an earlier survey trip to get the cattle safely across the parched centre. He'll need the stockwhip and the lasso before he finishes this journey—driving the cattle from one waterhole to the next. But although Chris Herrmann instils confidence with his conditioned reflex cry of 'no worries', cattle do die, and so do their calves on this tortuous trip.

The wheel has gone full circle in Australia's cattle industry: rising fuel and transport costs mean that the old-time cattle drover is in some circumstances a more economic proposition than the modern semi-trailer, especially during the cattle slump of the mid 1970s when prices fell dramatically. Drovers again began getting out their rusty, haunting Condamine bells, their horse hobbles and their tea billies, to reopen the great stock routes across central Australia.

Just a generation ago so many beef cattle passed along the great stock route from the Northern Territory into Queensland through the border town of Urandangie that western folklore had it that 'the dust never settles in 'Dangie'. In 1950, for example, a total of 122,212 head of cattle passed through 'Dangie in eight months—trudging through the flour-like soft red bulldust into Urandangie in the middle of Australia's Never Never, nearly five hundred kilometres south of the Gulf of Carpentaria. But by the end of the 1960s transport trucks had taken over completely and 'Dangie never saw a drover. Its population fell to its present seven (when everyone is at home)—including the owners of the hotel. Yet in 1974 at least four droving teams passed through, raising again the 'Dangie dust that had long since settled. And one of them was the first droving team anyone could remember heading from Queensland into the Northern Territory since beef cattle were first taken west to the Territory last century.

This story is about boss drover Chris Herrmann and his team of three Aboriginal and three white ringers who reblazed the overlanders' trail across central Australia, moving eight hundred head of Droughtmaster cattle, including sixty prize bulls, two and a half thousand kilometres from Richard Apel's Mimosa stud in southeast Queensland to his 5,500 square kilometre Nummery station on the edge of the Simpson Desert in the Northern Territory—as far as from London to Moscow.

Apel works out that by using staff labour as a droving team he can move the cattle for about $11,000 instead of $40,000 by semi-trailers, and by walking slowly and eating as they go they will arrive in much better condition than standing in fast-moving trailers. But on the other hand, they also stand to lose hundreds of head on the droving expedition if things go wrong.

The biggest risk is black gidgee poisoning—if cattle eat the leaves of the small black gidgee trees that are everywhere along the track it sends them raving mad and kills them. 'If they should take to the black gidgee we could lose fifty head and that's without stretching it. With cattle you always look on the optimistic side,' Chris Herrmann says. 'One bloke I heard of lost a hundred bullocks in one lot droving through here, to the black gidgee.'

Another ever-present problem is a cattle rush—or in TV language a stampede, but never did I hear that word out West. 'If a big mob of cattle hear a strange noise in the night they can be up and galloping within two paces and no fence will stop them. I've seen forty cattle killed in a rush,' says Chris Herrmann. In 1963 three hundred head from a mob of a thousand were staked by scrub timber or trampled to death in a 'terrible rush'.

But Chris Herrmann and Richard Apel have a plan to beat this threat. Packed in the four-wheel-drive Toyota are a couple of hundred metres of hessian and a pile of steel posts. Each night, instead of tired ringers on tired horses riding around the cattle (ringing them: thus the name ringers), Herrmann builds a big yard of wire, steel posts and hessian. No worries. Not that it would stop a rush—nothing will apparently. But the cattle can't see out, and as for noises, Chris Herrmann has his own unique solution. He places transistor radios on full volume on opposite sides of the cattle and sets them on an all-night radio station. 'That gives them a constant noise which drowns out any sharp crack,' he says. 'The biggest danger of a rush is in drummy country where the ground sounds hollow. You get a feeling about cattle after a while and ten to one these'll be all right.' But nevertheless we sleep with the Toyota and the fire between us and the cattle.

Two other things are on Chris Herrmann's mind. Although the cows have been specially chosen because they are not due to calve, the journey could bring the calves on. And then there is the terrible prospect of bushfire.

Even before the cattle leave Mimosa stud for the big trip, problems start. One man who was to make the trip is thrown from his horse mustering the cattle and breaks some ribs. He can't go. Because Nummery station in the Territory is disease-free, the eight hundred head must have all ticks removed and be tested for TB and brucellosis, which causes cows to abort. Testing takes a full week, but because some were immunized when young they react and have to be retested—putting the whole operation a week further into the burning summer months of the Centre and making the journey that much more dangerous.

Normally cattle only move from the Territory into Queensland and to market, and not the other way. But Apel wants to build up a Droughtmaster stud herd indigenous to the Territory so he can supply disease-free stud or herd Droughtmasters locally and anywhere in Australia without the need for costly testing. He believes the Droughtmaster—a breed developed in Australia to have high heat tolerance and tremendous walking and foraging abilities—is the ideal beast for central Australia. It is five-eighths Brahman (the hardy Indian breed with the hump on the neck) which resists drought and disease so well. The rest is British Shorthorn: 'If they were pure Brahman you'd never round them up once you let them loose out here,' Chris Herrmann says.

The men set out from Mimosa with the cattle for the forty-eight-kilometre trip to the rail line at Ideraway, where the cattle will be loaded for the long journey via Townsville to Dajarra, in northwestern Queensland. Someone miscounts by a hundred head and three men must go bush looking for them. Half a day is wasted looking for cattle that are in fact with us all the time.

As the train pushes up the coast of Queensland to Townsville before turning west it is stopped every hour to make any cattle lying down stand up. That night one of the wagons catches fire when an axle seizes and the oil boils, but it is put out before the cattle panic and they are put into a new wagon—which costs an extra three hours.

A cow in one rail wagon goes down and can't seem to get up.

Cattlemen say if they lie down too long they lose their sense of balance or get stomped on. So Chris's son Rolly, who is leading the train section of the journey to Dajarra (where Chris is waiting), climbs in with all the cattle and is kicked several times. He tries to winch her up with a rope made from the girth off his saddle, his reins and bridle. The men are working frantically because railway men further up the coast at Mackay are about to strike—they want taxi fares to work. A strike could leave the cattle stranded. The ringers try an electric jigger to give the cow a shock; there is a loud yell from inside—Rolly got the full shock in the leg.

They leave the cow and continue to the first stop—the small town of Prairie in western Queensland—for a three-day rest. The cow has a dislocated hind leg and is destroyed. The arduous journey is also bringing on calves and already there are three that won't be born on Nummery station as was hoped. Normally the calves would be destroyed, but a man with milking cows takes them.

After eight days on the move the cattle arrive in Dajarra—the end of the rail line in western Queensland—and they rush out of the jolting wagons like a crowd leaving the movies. Dajarra is about as far west as you can go in Queensland—if you don't count the tiny outpost of Urandangie, almost two hundred kilometres farther west near the Northern Territory border. The cattle must pass through 'Dangie on their seven-hundred-kilometre march to Nummery ... and cattle have to be very good to average more than sixteen kilometres a day in these hot conditions.

The cattle and the horsemen and motorbike riders head out between the hills to try to find the old stock route and to get as far as possible through the difficult first section of stony hills. Rolly can't find any stock track so just heads west. The first bore is thirty-five kilometres out of Dajarra—like an oasis in the desert—and it is decided to try to make the water by nightfall. 'There's good water there,' says Chris. 'The bore's got taps on it like an elephant's mouth.'

The bore is a big windmill which plunges an iron rod up and down under the earth sucking up the underground water that abounds in central Australia. If there were enough of these bores there would be no water problem, but they cost around twenty-five thousand dollars each now out here in the Centre. In fact this is what the stock route is all about. It goes from one government bore to the next. The water flows into a round (turkey's nest) dam and from there into a cattle trough where the level is controlled by a float. There are few fences in these areas because cattle can't move much more than ten kilometres from a bore. The number of cattle a property will hold out here is determined to a great extent by the number of bores.

The water in the dam is cold and inviting, and when the hessian yard is built everyone has a swim. Chris Herrmann has—from years of yelling in the bush—an extremely loud voice, capable of causing pain to anyone too close. The ringers have forgotten to wash the backs of their horses and come in for a distant verbal lashing. We have only eleven horses and one is already limping. 'We should have four horses a man for droving and we only have two and a half. We can't afford to let them get sores on their backs from the saddles,' Chris says. Aboriginal stockman Robin Cobbo's son John is one of the ringers and there is a white jackeroo, John Kunze, too. 'John the blackfella, you wipe up, John the whitefella, you wash up ... no racial discrimination here,' Chris says. These names are to stick for the whole trip. Round the campfire Chris Herrmann, a Queenslander, tells about some of the rough-tough blokes he has met in the Territory. He is particularly fascinated by one character who has never worn shoes in his life. 'He even wears spurs on his bare feet.'

As he is to do almost daily on this trip, Chris mounts a horse with a man behind him and counts the cattle out. The eerie galah-breast redness of the central Australian morning with the silver moon dying in the opposite blue sky is broken only by his cries of 'hundred' as the man behind him counts off another hundred cattle. If too many are missing the horsemen will have to go back and look for them.

The cattle continue through giant red ridges topped with smooth red boulders or impregnable fortresses of rock. Two motorbikes go on ahead looking for the next bore—and can't find it. Everyone looks at Chris Herrmann, who consults the lines drawn in his green book: 'No worries. I know where I'm going. I got full with a surveyor once,' he reassures the crew. 'Ten to one it's over the second ridge ahead. Anyway, we'll know directly.'

Rolly has gone back east and his younger brothers Steve and Alex are suffering on their motorbikes. The spear grass is more than a metre high in places and its tiny arrow-like spears jab through their clothes and can even penetrate their boots. The tyres of the smaller motorbike keep going flat and an examination shows the spinifex needles are the cause. The motorbike men are anything but happy and the cattle are hard to move through the big spinifex. 'You don't feel them after a couple of days,' Chris Herrmann assures his men. 'They'll still be getting them out in six months,' he tells me. He goes looking for a track for the Toyota and I ask how long he'll be. 'I'll tell you when I get back,' he replies.

Even though it is still nominally winter, and cold at night sleeping on the ground in the open, it is very hot in the day. My nostril linings have dried out and my lips are cracked by the sun. No one else seems to be suffering, but then I can't drink as much water as they can. My first mouthful of bore water I spat out on the red dust and even after practice I can force down only a mouthful. Little do I know that farther out the water gets much worse. I tried to get some cordial in Dajarra but they didn't have any. Even the tea tastes bad and the oily scum on top which sticks to the side of the chipped enamel mug puts me off.

As we cross a rise Chris sees the bore, but I can't see it. I have not yet learned to spot these shapes in a land of grass and small twisted trees. Chris Herrmann looks out across the new open plain to the horizon: 'We're out of the mongrel country. Look, the Land of Plenty—plenty of spinifex, bulldust and borewater.'

Near the bore are yards which will hold our mob. 'A gift from that fella above,' says Chris. 'The bee's knees.' The view from the yards as the sun goes down is an uninterrupted 360 degrees of rugged red hills running in long ridges. The orange and red sunset looks like a bushfire on the horizon. Except for the distant cry of the drovers all is silent. 'Hoo, you beauties. Work up, work up!' 'Oi, oi.' 'Come on, you buggers.'

It's 8.30 p.m. and very dark when the cattle arrive by moonlight and thunder past me shaking the ground ... more than four hundred tonnes of moving meat worth over $100,000.

As everyone rolls out their swags by the yards under the big moon and heat their traditional quart pots (oval-shaped billies for tea), Chris is a bit unhappy: 'We wouldn't want to hit the old man spinifex too much or we'll never get through,' he says. Because of the rough ground two horses are lame; and one is sick. 'The way we're going we'll have to all ride the same horse,' he says.

Like an Arab caravan moving through the desert, we continue across central Australia, droving the red river of cattle from waterhole to waterhole. It is getting much hotter and the flies are starting to appear under a hot winter's sun that burns like a Gold Coast beach on Christmas Day. The next windmill sucking water miraculously from beneath the parched earth is fifteen kilometres away and yet it is just visible on the horizon. The tallest shapes in central Australia, they stand like giant sentinels guarding life in the Centre. They keep alive the cockatoos on the dead trees and the sheep-sized eagle-hawks nearby. The red-beaked finches that live around the bores don't bother to fly away; man doesn't harm them here. And because they fly so dangerously close, Chris Herrmann calls them 'brumby birds'.

One cow is lame and limping badly and Chris may cut a horseshoe in half for her cloven foot and shoe her. The men are pushing the cattle a bit hard and Chris yells: 'You're droving, not driving.'

'City people think droving is a flash name for driving,' he tells me. 'I don't care if it takes an extra week to get there—I want to make sure the cattle get there in good condition.'

Some clouds appear and this is a real worry. 'Any amount of rain at all and we'd have to leave the truck because of the bulldust. It's so deep I have my sixty-foot tape to measure it,' Chris says, and only half grins. He is also worried the men will get dysentery from the bad bore water, which could hold him up for two or three days. He has cornflour to bind them up if necessary, and one ringer is already on it.

At the next bore, the cattle fight to drink around the float because they know that is the new water and the coolest. They always run the last kilometre because they can smell the water.

A man building a new trough tells me I should find and interview Territory Jack. 'He's a real, typical Aussie. Hard-drinking, a rough bony fella who tells big stories and whose trousers hang down the back and whose wife beats him with a stick. A real, typical Aussie.'

'The bikies,' as Chris calls his teenage sons Steve and Alex, have to clean the dust out of their air filters and fix more punctures. Steve can run rings around a horse, and rides flat-out through the open country. Some bumps send him into the air but always he stays on. 'I wouldn't be without the bikies,' Chris says. 'But you have to have good horses.'

Chris decides he must shoe one of the lame horses to try to fix her up. He gets out a hammer, a file and nails, and horseshoes with as many sizes as a set of golf clubs. He picks a pair that will fit and grabs the horse by the leg and holds the hoof between his knees. After a tug-of-war with the horse in which he loses his hat he holds the leg steady and with two hands begins to file the hoof. When it is level he files a niche in the back where the shoe fits and begins to drive six chisel-shaped nails into the hoof. The nails are shaped to bend outwards as they go in. When they protrude out the top several centimetres they are broken off. Putting in the two side nails is very dangerous. Once through the hoof the nails stick out the side and if the horse pulls his leg back through between Chris Herrmann's thighs he will be badly cut. It is a common accident, he tells me, and that is why he first establishes with the horse—by words and actions—that he is the stronger of the two.

The others are circling the cattle all afternoon while the tired beasts rest and feed. Making tea in the shade of a tree Chris Herrmann tells of his life in the bush and why he loves it. It all comes back to the oft-repeated: 'There's no one to 'noy ya—no salesmen, no religious cranks.'

Because the water makes even the tea taste bad I prefer Milo. So I must get some water before the tea leaves are dropped in and the pot lifted quickly from the fire and kicked with size eleven boots to settle the leaves to the bottom. Chris Herrmann always casually lifts the boiling billy out of the flames, puts his bare hand underneath, and tips the water into waiting mugs. He has a gentle quality when not working and talks softly and with plenty of dry bush humour. When washing-up time comes he tells of the fellow he once knew who had one lot of utensils and a dog. 'The dog was to lick the utensils clean,' he says. He tells how dry it can get in the Territory and how one fellow's property in a drought could only support two black cockatoos and four kangaroos—'and he had to move the kangaroos on to another bore'. At dinner Steve is making a stew and complains the corn beef smells a bit. 'In that case put it in quick,' says Chris.

That night flying cobweb strands with white eggs attached blow across the desert above the camp and wrap themselves around the Toyota aerial in their gleaming hundreds. I watch them pass above my swag in the moonlight. There are many kangaroos around, and an emu that easily ducks under a barbed-wire fence. There are hundreds of cockatoos, galahs and finches that live around the bores, and wild brolgas that seem to dance in panic.

The water at the next bore is so good that Chris lets out the bad water from the previous bore and it disappears without trace down a small crack in the red ground.

'I thought ten-to-one we would have to scrape the green stuff off the top,' Chris says of the good water. Over tea, while the rest of Australia discusses inflation and the budget, everyone here is talking about Birdsville disease—which could kill the horses if they eat a certain plant.

Chris spots a bull he doesn't like and takes the stern attitude some people in the cities adopt toward Treasury economists: 'The first thing we do when we get to Nummery is cut him. With bulls you always keep a sharp knife handy, it's better to cut too many than too few.' He and his sons discuss how much they enjoy eating the results of castration: 'I haven't eaten balls for weeks,' laments Chris over a corned beef sandwich. They taste like brains, I'm told.

Robin Cobbo, with eyes like a hawk, spotted three cattle we lost off yesterday's dinner camp. I mention that there don't seem to be any snakes around and he smiles: 'I saw five snake tracks today.' A sobering thought for someone sleeping in the open each night. Asked about snakes, Chris says he has never run into many. 'My wife would've killed more snakes than me. I wouldn't have had more than twenty arguments with snakes in my life.'

The bread we have is going bad but Chris insists 'It's just getting a few whiskers. Put it on the fire and burn them off.'

Big local bullocks break into our mob despite attempts to keep them out. Robin skilfully follows the biggest one through our cattle, slowly enough not to upset them. It is wild and big but he keeps cutting it off, even when it turns on him. The bullock weighs over half a tonne.

The rumble of the cattle gathering speed to the water is drowned out now by the big Condamine bells hung from the necks of our 'outlaw' horses. Robin is aged sixty and on the ground can hardly walk. He has a cramped stance from years in the saddle but on a horse he makes the riders in the cowboy movies look like rank amateurs as he and his horse pirouette, with Robin above wielding his big whip.

There are skeletons of dead cows at the next bore. This bore is called Cook's Well and Urandangie is now very close. Flies are a constant annoyance to me. 'Haven't noticed any,' says Chris. 'These few, they're just for company.' Flies are all over the corned meat but Chris says not to worry. 'These won't eat it all and if it gets blown you just knock the grubs off.' Chris chooses to wash from the cattle trough because the water is warmer than in the tank.

It is 11 p.m. and my turn to watch, and as Chris Herrmann gets into bed he remarks: 'If it was bullocks we were watching I'd sleep with my boots on.' The wireless, as everyone here so rightly calls it, is playing an appropriate number by Slim Dusty about the 'old drovers having black tea and damper by a fire of gidgee coal'.

'What would I do anyway if the cattle did rush?' I suddenly ask.

'If they come this way, wake me first,' is all the advice Chris gives.

It is so relaxing sitting by the flames that it is hard to stay awake.

There's nothing to do except stoke the fire. Walking around the yards I sing constantly (under instruction) to let them know I'm there. After the hour I follow standard procedure of not giving the next man—John the Blackfella (John Cobbo)—the watch until he is out of bed.

The horses are normally caught and saddled before the first red light appears, but the sun is up and a big white mare is still eluding capture. Someone forgot to hobble her front legs. Chris is upset and bursts into the yard himself and corners the horse—using his voice—after it has been eluding four men on foot.

A big white Brahman cow is wobbling as she walks and for kilometre after kilometre doesn't look as if she will go another step as she trails behind the pack. 'You'll be surprised how long a Brahman like that will keep going,' says Chris. But he says he might have to leave her behind near water if she falters any more.

Now it is grasshoppers, swarm after swarm of countless millions, that keep coming, tacking into the wind in search of more grass. 'If they get too nasty I'll take the stockwhip to the bastards,' says Chris.

At the top of the hill the cattle have made no progress and are almost blotted from view by grasshoppers.

We abandon dinner camp and go back to find the cattle actually stopped in their tracks by insects. The leaders are tossing their heads in annoyance and backing into cattle behind them. Despite all efforts of the drovers—who are flat-out staying on their horses—the cattle will not walk over the thick layer of grasshoppers. 'I'll bore it up 'em,' says Chris, wheeling his Toyota in front of the cattle. In low gear he clears a path in front, sending grasshoppers into the air like ash from a raging fire. Where he can't drive he walks, cracking his stockwhip and yelling abuse at the grasshoppers.

Four hours later the grasshoppers have gone—and we are just a few kilometres out of Urandangie. A car loaded with two families heading toward us from 'Dangie pulls up: 'How far to Urandangie?' the driver asks. They have driven through the place where it was said the dust would never settle, and they have missed it.

A cow has an early calf during dinner camp, and we are still not a quarter of the way through the drove. It is a little red bull calf. Chris talks to it nicely for a while, says nothing to me, and walks to the Toyota and gets out the axe. Still talking in a soft voice to the calf he raises the axe high above his head. I look away and thump! The calf is dead. Chris stands, hands akimbo, looking down: "Poor bastard," he says and walks back to the truck. This is not the last time he has to do this.

The boards at the 'Dangie pub wobble as we walk in. There are only stools for four. Everyone gets a different-shaped glass. Alice Springs and Birdsville are supposed to be the Back of Beyond in Australia but this is really it. Only two of the buildings in 'Dangie are occupied. The main streets are Margaret and Hutton but the woman in the pub doesn't remember which is which.

This is a town that once had eighty children at its school. There are no familiar water tanks on the buildings out here because it so rarely rains that tank water would be useless. So the town has a windmill bore. The news is that the next bore, nearly forty kilometres out of 'Dangie, is out of water. "We can't get to the second bore without water," Chris Herrmann says.

We make camp on the finish line at the 'Dangie racetrack. Considering that seven miles (eleven kilometres) a day was once regarded as normal droving and ten miles (sixteen kilometres) was fast, we have done very well. We have covered the hundred and seventy kilometres here in just seven days, with a late start the first day. 'It's the exotic breed,' says Chris. 'You wouldn't walk pure British cattle like this.'

Steve makes another flour-and-water damper for dinner—which is even better than the home-made bread from the woman at the hotel. We are near the Territory border now and Chris laughs about the long dingo fence built the entire length of the border. 'They built the fence to keep the dogs out but the gate is open and broken. Ten to one it has been like that for forty years. They spent millions but neither the fence nor the road are worth two bob,' he says. And he's right.

Next day a cow is reported lying dead in the yard. It calved during the night and the little calf crawled away into the shade. Some horses lick up the after-birth and the cow doesn't move. Chris gets out his rifle this time and walks solemnly toward the cow. He kicks the cow first—and it moves. He puts the rifle down and pulls the cow's back legs under its body. Then he takes a good hold on its ears and strains mightily to pull it to its feet. Sweating and swearing and with muscles standing out like steel cables, he gets the huge cow into a sitting position, but it falls across the other side and lies just as still. The struggle continues, using a spare wheel as support. Somehow Chris Herrmann gets the cow to its feet. And it recovers.

'Dangie is on the Georgina River and there are some deep waterholes left which we must avoid because they might bog the cattle. Chris must go and look at a safe way across and check the water at the next bore while the cattle have a rest day in 'Dangie. 'What bridge do we go over?' I ask. 'There are no bridges across the Georgina,' Chris replies.

We are on the so-called 'Plenty Highway'—and the fine bulldust is up to the axles most of the way. There is a bit of water at the mill but not much. 'They can have a sip,' says Chris. There are yards for the cattle, too, but they stink from dead beasts. 'That? That's no worries,' says Chris. 'We can live here.'

Another cow is calving, but the calf is caught with only its head and one leg out. The calf looks dead and the men are worried that if it stays in it will swell and kill the mother. Chris gets his lasso this time, rather than axe or rifle, and lassoes the calf and pulls it alive from the mother. He remarks, 'He'd make a bloody good bull calf,' and gets the axe.

Once again I look away as it swings down on the calf's head. How can he do it? 'I don't like doing it, but still and all someone has to do it. It's a job that has to be done. If we were closer to home we would leave the mother and calf and come back—or throw it on the trailer. Out here it would never survive alone.'

There is a two-day limit on holding cattle here and we must leave the next day. Chris looks gaunter and leaner than usual: two horses are lying down on the track not feeling well, the big white cow is to be left out alone for the night and seven bulls have taken a fancy to the one cow. 'That's bad. They can keep chasing her around and can kill her,' he says.

Chris measures many things in chains—'The sun's still got four chains to go,' he says when someone suggests they get the cattle in. I protest that there's no door to keep the bulls out when someone suggests we sleep the last night in the shed in the cattle yards instead of the open.

'I'll sleep across there,' says Chris. 'That'll frighten them off.'

We pass through the dingo fence into the Territory and the men are too tired to cheer. Steve crashes at speed into a deep hole and his motorbike breaks clean in half. This is disastrous because only eight of the eleven horses are still fit enough to ride. We are getting close to half way and the journey is beginning to take its toll of the weaker cattle. The big white Brahman cow can hardly move and is left at the bore. Maybe one day they will be back to get her ... if she is still here.

At Manners Creek, Chris shows his skill by welding the motorbike together and then killing a giant two-metre brown snake at the bore. He decides two lame cows and four small weaners which are trailing the mob must be left. Another calf must be killed. With the weaker cattle dropped off, the big mob is making between twenty-four and thirty-two kilometres a day. Half-way point on the drove is reached in fifteen days, way ahead of schedule. Around the campfire the men are jubilant as they eat their damper, jam and corned meat. Including the ten days to reach Dajarra they have been on the go for nearly four weeks.

They have been beside the dusty so-called Plenty Highway for four days but have seen no vehicles. Even Chris admits that the bore water our here is 'bloody awful'. And they say the next two are undrinkable. At a place called Beenleigh bore the cattle go thirsty for the night. The trough has a hole in it and all the water has run out. This does not help the cattle and three days later another cow and weaner must be left behind. Two more horses are limping through the spinifex as the men turn south down around the Simpson Desert and only six horses are now shouldering all the work. No one talks much—they just push on toward Nummery station.

They should be there in ten days if the cows keep going. Most are strong and fit and ready to run but some have diarrhoea from eating a certain type of weed and are weak. Two more must be left behind at the next bore. Luckily the weather has turned cold and it helps everyone. At Dinnara bore Chris decides to spell the cattle for a day. Incredibly it pours rain for two days. It is like seeing snow in Darwin. At first the rain is welcomed but everyone gets wet and miserable on their horses. Steve tumbles in slippery conditions and appears to have broken his leg below the knee. It is swollen and tender. No doctors here. The horses are so tired that he must keep riding his bike with his leg strapped. He is worth two or three horses. The horses are walking with heads close to the ground and a few kilometres before a place called Dead Horse Rock the brown pony falls by the wayside.

Sandhills now: we are almost in the desert, but close to Nummery, which opens up on to the desert. Steve can't ride, his leg is too sore, and is relegated to cook. The heat after the rain brings out the flies which swarm like bees around the men's faces, beating them to the food. All this land and nobody else here. Nobody for days and weeks of travelling. No wonder Chris laughs when he calls this a land of plenty. No wonder everyone else is hugging the shoreline near Manly and St Kilda and Surfers. No wonder politicians never come out here where there's only bore water, damper and corned beef.

Chris spots a grey mare near a pack of roos. 'We're near now. She got away from me in the desert six weeks ago. A good horse but I'll never get her back out here.'

In Chris's own words 'the flies are getting bigger and better every day'. It's now well and truly summer out here and everyone is finding the last few days hard work. The drove is down to four horses—the rest are just too weary to be ridden any more. But the men are all smiles and talk as they did when they first set out.

'Just as well we had Droughtmaster cattle with all that Brahman in them,' says Chris, with eight kilometres to go. 'I don't think any other breed could have walked that distance and put on weight in the time we took.' As he talks one of the sixty prize bulls breaks a leg and must be shot.

The seven-hundred-kilometre drove through the Centre is completed in just twenty-eight days' travelling and three rest days—an amazing average of more than twenty kilometres a day. From the eight hundred head the losses are one bull and two cows from accidents, the white cow and the pony which will almost certainly die. Six calves have had to be killed, three have been given away, and five cows and five weaners left behind.

Not a bad result considering the total length of the trip—from southeast Queensland deep into the Territory. For the owner, Richard Apel, there has been a saving of $29,000 over road transport. 'With that sort of result we might all go back to droving,' he says.

Somehow, though, I think I might stick to being a city slicker.

THE RIGHT POLITICS

THE OLD BOYS RUNNING QUEENSLAND

Queensland can be better understood if it is realized that, at the end of the 1970s, the state was ruled by ten people—all with remarkably similar backgrounds; backgrounds not shared by the vast majority of Australians.

The Bjelke-Petersen ten were all men: nine were farmers or graziers and the other was on a cane growers' executive before entering politics. They all left school years before they could be challenged by the complexities of tertiary study. All came from small Queensland towns or rural areas—what most Australians would call the bush. These ten men had by far the highest average age of any state government in Australia—over sixty years. That put them, on average, thirteen years older per man than the Fraser cabinet in Canberra. In mid-1979, only one of the ten was under fifty-eight, an age when most Australians are thinking about retirement.

On average, their lives began during World War I: in the days when Germany was ruled by a Kaiser. Their youth was gone by World War II. Generally, they married and had children—not in the difficult 1970s, not in the prosperous sixties, not even in the fifties when Bill Haley turned the world upside down forever by introducing rock and roll—but in the 1940s, the decade of the foxtrot and the gypsy tap.

No wonder then that the official Queensland view of the world has so often been archaic, expressing conservative and simplistic views of complex issues.

Their hometowns read like a tourist guide to rural and outback Australia: Ingham, Kingaroy, Emerald, Oxenford, Mackay, Gympie, Jandowae, Roma, Gayndah, Theodore. Their interests (listed in the official Queensland parliamentary handbook) covered scouts, flying, fishing, horse-racing (three times), football (four), bowls (four), cricket (two), golf, trots, Rotary, and one even listed 'sugar'. About the closest any got to something approaching higher culture was the tourism minister Max Hodges, who listed gardening.

The occupational backgrounds of Joh's top ten were hardly those of the average Australian, even the average Queenslander. Before entering politics two were sugar cane farmers, two were graziers, four (including Joh) were assorted farmers, and one a farmer-grazier. That adds up to nine. The one 'outsider' was Val Bird who produced the only job qualification resulting from formal study—mechanical fitter. But this took him (via mechanical harvesting) into the Ayr District Sugar Cane Growers' executive. Bird became education minister.

University students in Queensland sitting around discussing Shakespeare or George Orwell or Andrew Marvell ('The Grave's a fine and private place, but none I think do there embrace') are in a different world altogether. In fact, Marvell—if he were to be discovered by the stalwart ten—might find himself finally banned (three hundred years after his death) for telling his coy girlfriend: 'An hundred years should go to praise thine Eyes, and on thy Forehead Gaze. Two hundred to adore each Breast: but thirty thousand to the rest.' As an example of just how far behind the times was this Queensland cabinet, it should be pointed out that Marvell himself became a politician.

It was the banning of magazines like the American *Playboy* and the re-censorship of films already allowed into Australia that amazed Australians outside Queensland, and many within the state. But it was in line with the thinking of the Queensland top ten. Men in their sixties from the farm, with an average of four children (none less than three), and all with religious backgrounds are hardly likely to be impressed by the Playmate of the Month. Certainly not in public. And what pragmatic country person is going to be impressed by someone who says he only buys *Playboy* to read the articles?

Other anti-intellectual, anti-cultural attitudes sprang from the same limited range of interests: the belief that something was wrong with anyone who wanted to sit around all day reading, or painting or writing poetry, or even just enjoying the natural environment rather than trying to exploit it for profit. Naturally they condemned trade unions whose fights for wages and conditions traditionally were at the expense of the farmer and the grazier and the businessman.

The notorious ban on certain street marches seems to sum up the approach to life of these men. The ban, it should be remembered, arose after demonstrations by university students for a bigger weekly government allowance—better known by the acronym TEAS. So here was a group of 'radicals' seeking more of the taxpayer's money to study things that Queensland's rulers knew nothing about and therefore doubted the value of.

Some people advanced the argument that these ten men did not exclusively rule Queensland—that they did so only as part of an eighteen-man cabinet which included much younger men, some with university degrees, and some from the capital city, Brisbane. But that was ignoring the realities of the situation. While it was true that Queensland was ostensibly ruled by an eighteen-man cabinet, that cabinet also included ten from Joh Bjelke-Petersen's National Party. And true to their background and beliefs these men voted as one.

These then are the men who ruled Queensland (as at the middle of 1979)—the ten National Party cabinet ministers in Queensland:

Johannes Bjelke-Petersen, premier of Queensland since 8 August 1968. First elected to parliament on 3 May 1947—more than thirty years ago. A highly successful politician, having seen his party vote rise from 180,000 in 1972 to 291,000 in 1977. Now the longest serving Queensland premier ever. At sixty-eight he is well past normal retiring age and already others among the ten are eyeing his top job.

Chief among these contenders is **Russell James Hinze**, local government minister. Even at fifty-nine he is one of the youngest of the ten, but more importantly he is the only National Party cabinet minister in an electorate which is anything like urban. And this in a party trying to move into city areas. He is the member for the South Coast, a Gold Coast seat which takes in surrounding rural areas as well. He is notorious for his outspoken statements which have made him the best known National Party minister after Joh—though his pronouncements have an even blunter edge than Bjelke-Petersen's. On a *Monday Conference* show Hinze recommended not only castration, but also amputation for sex offenders. Since then he has announced that he mourned the passing of canvas seats in cinemas because that was where he 'learned to make love'. Recently accused some Aurukun Aborigines of being 'dropouts' and blamed 'bloody Poms' for much of Australia's industrial unrest. Chairman of the Gold Coast trots.

Ronald Ernest Camm, as mines minister since March 1965 the man behind the Queensland moves in the last thirteen years to mine and sell everything that can be sold. At one stage—during Bjelke-Petersen's shaky early years—Camm looked like becoming premier. Still hoping, but his hopes are fading with every month that Joh continues. Now sixty-four. A quiet man who has used the media shrewdly via a good press secretary. A sugar cane farmer born in Emerald.

Neville Thomas Eric Hewitt, the second youngest at fifty-eight, a grazier from Theodore. A man who likes to stay out of the limelight, rarely heard from and less ambitious than others. Once a close supporter of Joh Bjelke-Petersen—although clashing more with him now. Loves horse racing. When he was minister for Aboriginal affairs eight years ago an Aborigine on Thursday Island asked him in a bar to step outside for a moment to discuss something. The Aborigine then knocked Hewitt down. The minister laid no complaint.

Kenneth Burgoyne Tomkins, the hottest tip in government circles for Joh's job. A grazier from Roma, he became a minister four years ago after only seven years in parliament. Now holds important transport portfolio. Luckily for him few people know he was born down south—in Sydney. Now sixty-one.

Thomas Guy Newbery. Was minister for police during the Whitrod controversy and lost this sensitive portfolio at the next reshuffle. Now minister for culture, national parks and recreation. A sugar cane farmer from Mackay in North Queensland. Not very well known for a man in his position. Now sixty-four.

Valmond James Bird, the youngest by far at fifty, and the newest National Party minister. Holds important education portfolio. Originally a mechanical fitter who became secretary of the Ayr Cane

Growers' Executive. With the cluster of nine men a decade older than him he will be in a good position if his party kicks on in the 1980s.

Allen Maxwell Hodges, Max to most people. Lost position and influence when publicly sacked as police minister for backing his friend Ray Whitrod (who later resigned as police commissioner, saying there were signs Queensland was moving in the direction of a police state). Shunted to the tourism portfolio and little heard from since. A former secretary-manager of the Gympie Fruitgrowers' Association and dairy farmer. Now sixty-one.

Victor Bruce Sullivan, a farmer from Jandowae, aged sixty. A minister for ten years, he has specialized in primary industries since 1972. Little heard of in the capital.

Claude Alfred Wharton, sixty-four, minister for the big money portfolio of works and housing. Perhaps the Queensland minister with the widest range of interests: a former dairy, citrus and small crops farmer who also was a grazier breeding stud cattle as well as pigs.

One of the National Party's biggest problems is that although their vote has been increasing, they are mostly attracting the older voters. And with nine of their leading ten rapidly approaching or past retirement age, clearly the party needs some new young blood in cabinet.[1] The age difficulty the National Party faces stands out markedly when it is considered that the ALP leader, Ed Casey, is five years younger than the youngest National Party minister—and the Liberal leader, Dr Llew Edwards, at forty-three is even younger. And each month the situation seems to worsen for the National Party. The party did surprisingly badly in the 1978 Sherwood by-election, polling only 10.5 per cent of the vote, and the debacle over the pulling down of the historic Bellevue Hotel in 1979 lost the party many more potential supporters, especially in Brisbane.

There is however another generation of younger men who could be brought into cabinet. Like Mike Ahern from the town of Maleny, who at thirty-six and a Bachelor of Agricultural Science, would add

1 In the second half of 1979 two of the ministers—Hodges and Newberry—were in fact replaced by younger men.

some balance. Though young, he has been in parliament ten years. He does face the drawback however of being a Catholic in a party of WASPS.

Lin Powell, thirty-nine, should be at the top of the list, but he isn't because he has been prepared to buck his party on some old ideas and because—as a teacher—he gives a different view from that of the farmers. He has made himself very popular in what was once a Labor electorate.

A man who fits the party image more is a forty-four-year-old grazier, born in Charleville: Neil Turner. His rugged looks, and ability to talk simply, helped him overcome a 14 per cent deficit to win the western seat of Warrego from Labor in 1974. He is a man to watch.

As Queensland turns the corner into the 1980s, however, Bjelke-Petersen's ruling National Party gerontocracy looks as entrenched—and out of date—as ever.

MOONBI'S BULLDOG

John Sinclair wears a massive bulldog on his T-shirt. Not that he really needs the label. For six years he fought international sand-mining companies, real estate developers and timber-getters for Fraser Island. His success was staggering: by October 1976 a federal inquiry recommended the banning of virtually all sandmining on the island, which was called Moonbi by the Aborigines.

It was because of him that a federal government group inspected Fraser Island in June 1975 for a full week as a prelude to the two-month public inquiry into Fraser Island land uses.

All this followed his successful appeal to the High Court in May 1975 against a mining warden's decision to allow five new sand-mining leases on the island. Sinclair had lost in the mining warden's court and lost in an appeal to the Queensland Supreme Court, but he hung on.

Sinclair, on the face of it, was an unlikely candidate for the title of Australia's greatest-ever conservation fighter. He left school early, lived in the small, conservative city of Maryborough and wore his hair short-back-and-sides under a broad-brimmed bush hat. He lived in a small wooden house and drove a 1957 model Holden. But he fought a fight to preserve Fraser Island the like of which had not been seen before. In 1970 he formed the Fraser Island Defence Organization (FIDO) and made a bulldog called Fido its symbol. Since then he has shown all the qualities of his chosen standard: a refusal to take a step back, a vice-like grip on his adversaries, and a daunting appearance. For Sinclair is built more like a bullock than a bulldog. He is six feet and sixteen stone with a massive head like a tomahawk—big nose slicing forward. His face is more a statement than a question, reflecting immediately his mood changes.

His fight brought him more deprivations than most crusaders

suffer. Maryborough people saw the sand-mining and timber-getting as their only real future and so to them Sinclair was a threat. Worse, because he was a Maryborough man born and bred. Sinclair admits that he and his wife Helen lost close friends. 'My wife has lost her best friend over this. The friends I have lost I no longer regard as having been friends.'

We were talking in a tent one night during the inspection by members of the 1975 inquiry.

Sinclair cared enough to take a week's holiday to be with the inquiry to show his side of the island. Then he took his long-service leave to attend the inquiry every day.

Sinclair left school at fifteen, but he studied hard and returned to Gatton Agricultural College to get a diploma in agriculture. Then he became an adult education officer and completed an economics degree at Queensland University by correspondence. In 1969 he was one of Maryborough's bright young sons and was sent as a Rotary exchange student to the United States.

He was warned many times to stop his campaign and suffered some painful moments. At the height of the controversy one garage displayed a sign which read: 'Sinclair not served here'. At the Maryborough Show he led his young scout troop into the ring and was loudly booed by the crowd.

Sinclair himself is like an overweight boy scout. As the inquiry trudged across the island, he led the way in bare feet, wearing a pair of shorts and his bulldog T-shirt, a big knife slung on his hip like a six-gun, and a big hat on his head. He contrasted markedly with the inquiry team in their long trousers and shoes and, on some days, ties. He seemed always to be chopping firewood, digging holes or lighting lanterns for the southerners. This was obviously much more his environment than theirs.

When it was the turn of the sand-miners or forestry workers to show the inquiry their operations, it was Sinclair who stood his ground and tried to poke holes in their arguments. He was more inquisitive than aggressive, answering rebuffs only with more difficult questions.

One day the sand-miners took the inquiry to an experimental plot used by the foresters. A spokesman explained to the inquiry that the land had been cleared and burnt and a foot of topsoil removed. The topsoil was kept for a month and then respread and fertilized. Now there were many plants and bushes growing. It seemed very impressive.

Then up spoke Sinclair: 'I would point out that the heaviest applications of fertilizer were put here at the top and we must move through to the back to see the poor parts.

'Also'—jumping on to a huge stump—'you will notice there are lots of stumps on this block, which means a total removal of topsoil was impossible and therefore it is not a good reproduction of sand mining.

'And the biggest difference, I would argue, is that the bed of sand beneath was not disturbed as it is in sand-mining to a great depth and the minerals removed.'

When the foresters showed their handiwork they came to a burnt-out patch.

Sinclair: 'Is this one of your deliberate fires?'

Forester: 'This was a wildfire. Check your facts.'

Sinclair: 'Was it treated to eliminate satinay and encourage blackbutt?'

Forester: 'No, we don't burn satinay [a giant rainforest tree]. It was a tourist fire. I don't know if it was a FIDO fire.'

Sinclair: 'Is it not true that eucalyptus like blackbutt are favoured by fire rather than rainforest trees?'

Forester: 'A fire would occasionally be necessary to retain them as eucalypt types. This forest would be heading to a climax as a rainforest form. We are holding the forest in its present condition.'

Sinclair: 'Holding back nature?'

Forester: 'What is nature?'

The conservationists, headed by Sinclair and Pat Mackie of Mount Isa fame, wanted the inquiry to spend a lot of time at beauty spots; the sand-miners and forestry men wanted them to see all their operations. This meant that the inquiry spent from breakfast to dark most days bouncing slowly along bumpy dirt roads huddled in Land Rovers. On an island one hundred and forty kilometres long and up to twenty-six kilometres wide, that means a lot of driving.

The conservationists believed that their opponents wanted to keep the inquiry exhausted and on the move so they would not get time to appreciate the beauty of the island. And certainly with the schedule that was set it could hardly have suited anti-conservation interests better. The inquiry members were exhausted—by the pace and by the prosaic approach to trips adopted by the companies.

It must have been very hard for the sand-miners and foresters to accept Sinclair into their midst during this time. For Sinclair was going to cost them untold millions of dollars. Dillingham-Murphyores had export licences for only two of their leases—and these alone involved contracts worth $43 million.

Sinclair began his campaign by producing his own newspaper about Fraser Island. This evolved into a two or four-page supplement to the area newspaper, *The News*, and copies were sent to five hundred FIDO members and conservation groups throughout Australia. Sinclair began issuing press releases like a professional public relations man, at the rate of one every couple of days. He produced other publications for distribution around Australia, such as *Fraser Island: Priceless Pearl or Political Pawn?*—with maps of all sand-mining leases (with lease numbers) and forestry operations. Pictures of clear-felled timber areas and sand-mining were included.

In June 1974 there was an ugly meeting in Maryborough. Sinclair's position in fact was so dangerous that locals say he was warned by fellow conservationists not to speak. And he didn't. Conservationists were shouted down by unionists in an ugly demonstration of the mood in Maryborough. When more than a thousand anti-conservationists turned up for a similar meeting in Maryborough a year later John Sinclair and his supporters again decided it was wiser to avoid a violent clash. Sinclair had to put up with people trying to have him sacked from his job in the Education Department, and he constantly received abusive phone calls.

To get more supporters Sinclair organized cheap safaris to the island to show people its beauty spots. Almost invariably he won a truckload of new supporters. It was Sinclair who got Dr Moss Cass, then minister for conservation, to see the island, which set off the inquiry.

Then came the Fraser Island song, written and sung by a Brisbane couple; it was pressed as a record in 1971 and sold out. When the issue became national, Sinclair organized a re-press. The song is unashamedly emotional:

> Who will rip this land apart?
> Who will sell my soul?
> How many bidders are waiting in line
> For the promise of easy gold?
> Who will tear my timber down
> And leave my wildlife dying?
> Is there no one left to care for me?
> My name is Fraser Island.

During the visit by inquiry members in 1975 Sinclair told me: 'Whenever I wonder if it is worth the struggle I just have to spend an hour at Wabby Lakes or stand for a moment in Rainbow Gorge. Some places have a magic which really revives and gives new energy. There are many places here which are like cathedrals. It is a feeling of renewal. Did you notice how when we walked back from the enchanted valley not a soul spoke? Nobody even wanted to. You just feel as if you have just communicated with your soul.

'I guess I am like the Man of La Mancha: I dream the impossible dream, to beat the unbeatable foe.'

When I arrived at Sinclair's home after the inquiry week, his wife sat at a dining table which was smothered in letters of support. Unsolicited donations from around Australia that week totalled $1000, and $750 the previous week. The letters kept John Sinclair going.

He had other successes, as well as setbacks, in his six-year struggle. In 1974 he managed to split 200 Murphyores shares into single units, making 200 FIDO members shareholders in the company. He reasoned that this way his members would cost the company money because each would be entitled to an annual report and tiny dividends. Shareholders also could ask questions at the annual general meeting of the company. When there were reservations by the stock exchange over the technicalities of dividing shares into units of one, Sinclair demanded that the shares be suspended until the matter was resolved. It was resolved.

In August, 1973, FIDO received a great boost when it managed to get the Inquiry into the National Estate to visit the island.

But Sinclair's real success stemmed from his ability to generate publicity. Federal cabinet was subjected to a stream of telegrams from him. His newsletters, always filled with photographs, even listed such things as sand-mining company staff changes, bulldozer sizes, rates of sand-mining, and the extent of subsidies to timber millers.

Sinclair decided to fight the sand-miners after he discovered that mining had been granted on the island without people knowing. 'Oh, they did put in one miserable advertisement giving datum pegs and compass bearings in a way that people would never know. Thus there was no hearing for the first leases in 1966. The public interest was not even considered.'

After that Sinclair appeared in every case. Twice FIDO's barrister was unavailable and, with no money available, Sinclair took the job himself—once, in August 1973, cross-examining sand-miners in the warden's court for three successive days.

One thing in particular that worried Sinclair was that the beautiful lakes perched high above the sea in crusty sand would drain if the foredunes were dug up. So on the last day of the inquiry he took everyone on an hour-long hike from the beach into the sandhills to the beautiful Wabby Lakes. The lakes are up to twenty-five metres deep with white sandy beaches one side and thick bush around the rest.

After twenty minutes of walking through ferns and bush, we emerged on a desert stretching and widening before us as through an arch: in the middle, some yellow sand, to the right some brown, and far off a patch of brilliant white. There were a few lonely, stark sentinels of what had once been mighty trees—now etched to delicate driftwood by the ceaselessly moving sand.

As we struggled across that open blow to emerge at the edge of sheer sand drops down to Wabby's two green lakes I wondered what it might cost to try to reproduce such a scene.

Fraser Island is certainly a strange and fascinating area: the yellow-red sand pinnacles worn to a knife-edge by the winds; the Aboriginal middens marked by the pile of ugarie (local name: wong) shells; the natural champagne rockpool north of Indian Head; the black tortoises at Lake Bowarrady (Beauty Spot No 44, according to the sign) that come out of the water to eat from your hand. And Woongoolbver Creek, which leads like a white path through dense rainforest, past palm trees straight as arrows, enclosed overhead by the jungle. The sandy bed is covered by a foot of clear, cold water. Within the forest is the anglopteris fern, the oldest living fern in the world.

But John Sinclair doesn't walk there now. The man who saved it all, he was transferred hundreds of kilometres away by the state government as a punishment after the export of mineral sands from Fraser Island was banned.

WHITE MAN WITH A BURDEN

The federal government became enmeshed in the Aurukun affair because of the power and reputation of one Queenslander—a man who is seen by many as a sort of great white chief of the state's Aborigines. The Aborigines here call this man 'long bones', because he is so tall—a strongly built, silver-haired man born fifty-five years ago in north Queensland and brought up in the small towns of Cooktown and Mareeba.

His name is Pat Killoran, a man who has received the ultimate honour of being 'adopted' by both Islander and Aboriginal families and who, I am informed, has personally fostered a number of Aboriginal children. He has worked for the Queensland Department of Aboriginal and Islanders Advancement for more than thirty years and has been director for the last fourteen. A public servant, he stays in the background—so much so that those Aborigines who oppose him call him 'the possum', because they say he never comes out in the light. But this does not mean he is not well known. Federal officials know him by his impressive public service title 'the Director', and he has immense powers conferred on him by the state Act, which covers the thirty-five thousand Aborigines on state reserves. Aborigines on both sides of the political or philosophical fence know him because he has worked among them for so long.

Those Aborigines who admire him believe he uses his wide powers for their good and has devoted his life to them; but those who oppose his methods see the convent-educated Killoran as their greatest enemy, a white man using a repressive Act to keep Aborigines down. Thus, when militant Aborigines demonstrated in the streets of Brisbane against the state Act in 1974, they did not demonstrate outside the offices of either Joh Bjelke-Petersen or the then minister Neville Hewitt, but rather outside the office of public servant Pat

Killoran. It was from this demonstration that the chant 'Kill Killoran' originated.

Killoran in fact was the man who precipitated the whole Aurukun affair. This happened back in October 1976 when, in his annual report to state parliament, he accused some Christian churches of replacing pastoral care 'with a philosophy of materialism and political bias'. With the release of that report the days of Uniting Church rule at Aurukun and Mornington Island were numbered.

Showing the difference between the philosophical ideal he was pursuing and that of the church (and Canberra), he argued that the Aborigines needed time, not pressure. He said there had been a marked decline in the moral and physical standards of some communities. 'Community residents have been left without spiritual guidance that is a basic necessity for any human being. At the same time, the Aboriginal community is seen as a fertile field for social experiment and investigation that would not be tolerated by any other sector of the population. It is a pity that many of those involved do not consider that they are dealing with people who are immensely sensitive and require the advantages of stability and time, rather than the status of social guinea pigs.'

Killoran said Aborigines were coming under pressure from people anxious to force upon them political, social or economic solutions to what non-Aborigines regarded as their problems. But one simple blanket solution was not possible. He listed what he called proposed 'outside solutions' to Aboriginal problems as decentralization, separate development, abolition of state legislation and acquisition of land through land rights.

Given these views stated by the Director of the Aboriginal department it is not surprising that eventually the Queensland government moved to acquire full control of the Uniting Church reserves. The Killoran statement led the then Presbyterian Church (now Uniting Church) Aboriginal liaison officer, the Rev. Gordon Cootes, to accuse Killoran of being politically biased. 'The policies of both the Liberal and Labour parties are in line with what we are doing in the missions. So Mr Killoran's comments can only be seen as political statements by a public official,' he said.

Certainly, Killoran's view of the best method of helping Aborigines is based on a philosophy different from that of the federal Labor or Liberal governments, and his view has framed the policy of his own state government. Killoran—who admittedly has great knowledge of the people and their way of life—wants them working and going to school, and is apparently unhappy at the church attitude which—in the words of one antichurch state official—'wants to see the Aborigines wandering around the bush living off goannas'. The Killoran attitude is in line with the state government policy of 'assimilation' for all of the state's fifty-five thousand Aborigines, the biggest state group in Australia.

Queensland is against land acquisition for Aborigines not so much for the stated reason that it would cause separate development but because the government is concerned that in the Northern Territory the Aborigines have been given mineral rights to their land as well. The state argument is that in Australia mineral rights are vested in the crown—that is, in the state government. And an individual in Australia who owns land is in no way entitled to own the minerals beneath it. Certainly the American Indians, as Canberra argues, own the minerals under their reservations—but Queensland counters that in America all freehold land owners have mineral rights. In Australia no one has—except Northern Territory Aborigines.

Anyone who has visited a reserve or a Torres Strait island with Killoran, as I have, could not help noticing his knowledge of the people and their way of life—and the reverence which many pay him. He appears to be regarded as something between a great white chief and a beloved father figure. But, on reading the Aborigines' Act and its regulations, it is obvious that Killoran is vested with wide-ranging powers over the lives of these people. Critics say such powers should not exist or, if they must, they would be better placed in the hands of the minister who has parliamentary and electoral responsibility.

The thing that stands out in the Act and its regulations is the number of times the 'Director' is referred to—more than a hundred times. Perhaps his most controversial powers are those under which he can, through his district officers, manage an Aborigine's property, savings and earnings—but only upon application by the Aborigine to have this done. In the words of the Act the district officer can then 'take possession of, retain, invest, sell or otherwise dispose of any of such property'—but only with the approval of the Director. Killoran can tell an employer of such an Aborigine to pay the whole or a specified part of his wages to the Director who can use the money 'as he deems fit' for the benefit of the Aborigine or his family. If an Aborigine who asks for his property to be managed should die the Director has power to administer the estate. And, if the benefactors cannot be established, it is the Director who can determine who is to benefit 'in order and proportions determined by the Director'. He can do this 'notwithstanding the provisions of any act or rule of law or practice to the contrary'.

The paternalistic state government sees this part of the act as being of benefit to the Aborigine and his family—and not too far removed from the white man's maintenance court orders. But the difference is that the Aborigine, once he has handed over control of his possessions, loses complete control of his affairs. If the Aborigine should apply to go back to spending his own money as he wishes, Killoran may allow this 'if he is satisfied that termination of the management will not be detrimental to the best interests of the applicant or of any member of his family who should be supported by him'. However the Director does not have the final say, because if he refuses to hand this right back he must within twenty-eight days ask the local magistrate to decide the issue. If the magistrate should refuse termination of the management the Director alone can continue to refuse the Aborigine's applications for a further six months. Also, if an Aborigine whose property is being managed is missing, the Director may 'at his sole discretion' operate the Aborigine's business and may sell any property—other than land.

Even in such everyday things as drinking beer and being married it is the Director who has the final say for the Aborigines on Queensland's reserves. If an Aboriginal couple have—although not married—been living in a traditional racial union they can get official blessing with a certificate from the Director saying they live together 'in accordance with recognized traditional racial practice'.

The Director conducts the supply and sale of beer on reserves, and, under the regulations, he can fix the days and the hours in which beer may be sold and consumed. But he cannot allow beer to be sold for more than four hours in twenty-four and no Aborigine can take beer from the canteen to drink it at home or elsewhere. The Director can also restrict the quantity of beer per person sold in any day on a reserve. (But state officials say this is in reality delegated to the local elected Aboriginal councils.) The Director must, however, discontinue the selling of beer if the Aboriginal council on the reserve says so. Aboriginal councils until 1975 consisted of three elected people and two appointed by the Director and the interests of the two groups were seldom at variance. Also, if candidates did not offer for election, or an election could not be held, all five could be appointed by the Director. Since 1975 however all five have been elected.

Critics of the Act say that because the election is administered and facilitated by the Director's representative—the department's district officer—he can influence who stands and possibly also the voting. They claim this is because voting is not compulsory and Aborigines with good ties with the district officer would be more likely to turn up at his office to nominate, and also to vote on polling day.

Perhaps the Director's greatest power is in having the final say as to who can visit or live on an Aboriginal reserve. Killoran, for example, can eject a person who is not entitled to be on a reserve 'with such force as is reasonably necessary'. The person does not have to be prosecuted first. The penalty for being on a reserve when not entitled is two hundred dollars. The Director or the chairman of the Aboriginal council can give a permit for an Aborigine to visit a reserve. If however an Aborigine desires to reside on a reserve for more than one month he needs a permit granted by the local Aboriginal council and the Director. This means the Director can veto the residence permit, but in practice the decisions are made by the councils.

The Director may, as the Act says, revoke a visitor's permit. He can also revoke a permit to reside, but first he must give notice in writing to the Aborigine to show cause why the permit should not be revoked. A copy of the notice must be given to the chairman of the Aboriginal council on the reserve. If the Director is not satisfied with the Aborigine's explanation the Aborigine must leave the reserve. But if an Aborigine does not get a permit to reside, or loses it, he can appeal to the local magistrate who can decide the issue. However there is no appeal against refusal of permission to visit. A key section of the Act, section twenty-four, says that in no case shall it be obligatory on an Aboriginal council or the Director to grant a permit to visit a reserve. Legal opinion is that this is an attempt to prevent anyone from taking out a prerogative writ in a court to compel this to be done—leaving complete discretion for visit permits in the hands of the Director, or the elected council.

The Director can also decide if an Aborigine is an aged, infirm or slow worker and then set a rate of wages for him less than the agreed award minimum. But first the Aborigine must apply to be considered in this category. In some circumstances this can be more humane than it sounds—allowing someone to work less than full-time or full-pace, and of course for less money.

Killoran controls the rules covering Aboriginal police forces on reserves, and, through the Aboriginal councils, has the ability in many cases to influence the laws and orders the councillors make for the communities. Every resident on or visitor to a reserve must obey all lawful instructions of the Director. The Director may 'of his own motion' cause to be made inspections, investigations and inquiries 'as touch upon matters material to the administration of the Act'. The Director or his delegate may enter and inspect any reserve premises if he first gets the consent of the occupier or a warrant from a justice. And when making an inspection or inquiry he has the power to question anybody on any matter, and every resident must answer all questions unless of an incriminating nature.

Anyone shocked by this should contemplate the fact that police have the same powers over all citizens, though on reserves the powers are vested in non-police officials.

Departmental district officers working on reserves must do as the Director orders, and his powers do not stop merely at those stated under the Act. The Act says he can exercise any powers that 'are necessary or expedient to effect the purposes of this Act'.

One fact emerges clearly from the verbose pages of legal jargon which presently rule the lives of two-thirds of Queensland's Aborigines. They do *not* have the same freedom as whites or Aborigines living off the reserves—and the extent of their freedom depends very much on one man: the Director.

Of course no Aborigine is compelled to live on a reserve if he thinks he can make it in the white man's world.

When it comes to mining on a reserve either the Director (as trustee) or the minister must approve the lease—not the local Aboriginal council. And this is where the Uniting Church clashed with the state government. The church and Canberra want mining rights vested in the Aborigines.

With such powers it is clear that the Director can stop relatives visiting each other on reserves or determine how long they can stay, he can keep radicals off reserves, make people have a written permit to live on their own reserves, decide how much they can drink each day, decide if a man is a slow worker, and decide who is incapable of managing his own financial affairs. This is not to say that the Director rigidly enforces all these powers—but they are there.

The Queensland government has been promising publicly to alter this Act for several years, but by late 1979 only minor administrative changes had been made. It is safe to say that while Queensland has such powerful men as 'Long Bones' Killoran in charge of Aborigines, reformers both within the state and in far-off Canberra will be hard pressed to win fights with Bjelke-Petersen's government on Aboriginal affairs.

POLICE TAKE TO THE STREETS

My most vivid recollection of the three-hour battle which turned central Brisbane into a civil war zone in October 1978 was that Johannes Bjelke-Petersen was not there to witness it. For had he been there in the thick of it he would know that he has helped create a monster which cannot be either imagined or adequately described: it has to be seen, and felt, to be believed.

The story is not told in repetitious reports of so many hundred arrests, so many convictions, so many allegations. It is told by the girl picking up the discarded thongs and sandals of arrested demonstrators in her overflowing upturned hat. It is told by the group of five police who charged into the crowd in the safety zone of the city square and pushed the front three rows out into the street where they could be arrested. Two senior police eventually had to pull these police back out of the crowd. It is told by the demonstrator held in a headlock against a van who was visibly shaking with fear—and still shouting insults, until the policeman threw him on the concrete of the Albert Street bus stand. It is told by the dilemma of the many police upset by the rough tactics of some of their fellows: as one demonstrator was punched into a van, a young policeman urged him to mind his head.

Some police even dodged out of the way as demonstrators surged again and again at the lines of police; yet one large policeman, his eyes beads of rage, dragged people from the footpath and manhandled them in every way without actually hitting them.

But the real story is the way anger grew as confrontation grew; the way two mainly peaceful sides grew first in anger, then in power, and then in violence. This is the lesson of the Brisbane battle.

At first the crowd was so peaceful and reticent that Senator Georges and Tom Uren could get only about fifty people to follow them up Albert Street—the street of cinemas in Brisbane. The marchers called to the crowd to follow, but many were reluctant to confront the massed lines of hundreds of police. The leaders who set off first in fact turned out to be the wise ones. They were peacefully apprehended, photographed and led into vans. Long-time demonstrator Dan O'Neill smiled and chatted with the policeman who stood beside him.

It was only as violence bred violence and inadequacy bred frustration that sections of the crowd turned into Queensland kamikazes, willing to charge alone and screaming into hundreds of police. The crowd's anger took two hours to come; two hours to break.

Those arrested beat loudly on the roofs of the police vans and the drum noise echoed from the City Hall, the Reserve Bank building, and the Commonwealth Bank building. As each van load left the crowd cheered; more were inspired to sacrifice themselves to their cause.

Two eggs flew across Adelaide Street at police in front of Wallace Bishops (the famous Brisbane jewellers) but, as usual, pre-demonstration stories of 'bags of stones' to be used by demonstrators proved false. There were no weapons, no stones.

Twice I was confronted by suspicious police as I took notes, but they backed off at the sight of my black Queensland press pass; one good thing about these demonstrations is the relative freedom of movement granted the press. A plainclothes policeman being named by a chanting crowd told a photographer not to take his photo and asked for the photographer's press pass. The photographer asked him for his police pass; they showed passes and backed off.

Upset by the lack of success of single demonstrators moving towards the police, a large section of the crowd surged through two rows of surprised police. Then came the headlocks and the arrests. Now the crowd was shouting 'The people will never be defeated!' A young woman had 'Assaulting Police' written on her 'field charge sheet'. As a man near her struggled for breath in a headlock because he wouldn't face the police camera she shouted: 'You are choking him, you bastards.'

'Slap a charge of obscene language on her too,' said a very angry policeman surrounded by the press and trying to hold his temper.

'Aren't you puritans,' she said.

It is a pity that people like Bjelke-Petersen and Liberal leader Edwards did not see, and feel, all this, did not stand in Albert Street and see people fighting—physically and at times hysterically. Perhaps if the politicians left their lofty offices and walked down past the Queensland Book Depot and saw the eyes of the people, and heard their cries, they would not so readily promote such confrontations.

IPSWICH'S FIDGETY FIGHTER

It was 1961 in the small Queensland city of Ipswich and a young, fresh-faced police constable was learning what it was like to feel the sting of Gough Whitlam's tongue. Whitlam, then deputy leader of the ALP, had driven in to Ipswich at the end of an arduous five-thousand-kilometre trip around Queensland—a journey that swung the state to Labor and went within a few votes of finishing the Menzies era.

The twenty-eight-year-old constable was the endorsed Labor candidate for the seat of Oxley, taking in Ipswich. He faced the job of unseating the federal health minister, Dr Donald Cameron. Leaning in at the car window, the constable told Whitlam that there had been a muck-up with halls and they could not have the one they wanted. A tired Gough Whitlam told the young candidate what he thought of him and his hall, little knowing that this man would one day be his successor as Labor leader.

The man whose head jerked back out of the car window was Constable William George Hayden, future Medibank man, federal treasurer and, perhaps, future ALP prime minister.

Though this was only a minor incident, it did reveal the background to the Whitlam-Hayden relationship—for the two men came to the top from opposite ends within the ALP. As a young man in Canberra Bill Hayden established himself as a radical with, some thought, outlandish views on how the country and its economy should be run. He was regarded throughout the 1960s as a left-winger and came very much under the influence of the Jim Cairns view of life: both were guided by principle and dedicated to idealism.

The son of an American merchant seaman who jumped ship and entered Australia as an illegal immigrant in the depression and found work eventually as a piano tuner, Hayden grew up in working-class South Brisbane (as I did)—then Vince Gair's stronghold. He left school at sixteen to enter the state public service as a junior clerk, but found filing papers so boring that at nineteen he left and became a policeman. In nine years with the force he saw the difficult side of life as a constable in small country towns.

When the Labor split came in 1965 he was at Redbank, near Ipswich, on the beat. He was also often to be found sitting in the Ipswich railway workshop cafeteria swotting up textbooks. He joined the ALP, kept studying, and made 1960 his big year. That year he matriculated, got his Labor pre-selection for Oxley and married Dallas, a coalminer's daughter from Ipswich.

Hayden burned with zeal in parliament, attacking all things Liberal and upsetting Sir Robert Menzies so much that in a moment of exasperation Menzies called him 'a poor little ignoramus'.

Unlike Whitlam, Hayden had some natural disadvantages to overcome. He is a smallish man with a high-pitched, sing-song voice—and, as Ming obviously judged, it was not going to be easy for Hayden to get to the top. The fact that he did succeed in a tough arena where image is at least as important as ability reveals something of the personality of this former police constable. It tells something of his tenacity that he got into politics the hard way—defeating, ironically, a federal health minister. In doing so he became the youngest member of federal parliament, at twenty-eight, and later he became the youngest minister in the Labor Party government.

During the 1960s Hayden's view of things changed—largely as a result of his study. In 1963 he started studying law after completing his matriculation at night school. 'But I soon realized that while lawyers could pull the structure of an act to pieces, the important thing was economic management,' he recalled in 1975 in the bedroom of his better than modest brick home in Ipswich—the bedroom being the only quiet room away from his three children and incessant phone calls. 'At that stage I was economically illiterate, and it was frustrating trying to work out what all those symbols meant.'

Unlike Whitlam, Hayden went in for economics and performed the very difficult feat of obtaining a Queensland University economics degree in just five years of night-time and correspondence study. This changed his view of life considerably and it was at this time that his friends started to note a moderation—a movement away from the policeman mould to a man who now has a reputation for 'seeing everything as grey rather than black and white'—as a fellow ALP politician put it. But he was still not really one of Whitlam's men—and in fact Hayden was one of Arthur Calwell's strongest supporters in the leadership showdowns with Gough.

In 1969 at a federal conference in Melbourne Hayden was saddled with Labor's Medibank pledge and he surprised even his own party by later taking on the powerful health funds and the medical profession and producing in government a Medibank system which worked. Hayden was probably the only man who could have done this—because even his enemies admit he is a very hard worker, a studious, well-organized person. But, over and above these qualities, Hayden apparently has another strength which could serve him well as a leader: he is, despite his reputation as a softie, able to make tough decisions.

In January 1977, for example, Hayden took on a job for the ALP convention that no one else wanted—for very good reasons. He brought down the report of the Appeals Committee, a report on people expelled from the party and refused endorsement. As a colleague said: 'No one particularly likes this because it is messy and you sometimes have to chop heads. But Bill Hayden was willing to take a tough job and do it better than anyone else had done.'

His close colleagues say Hayden has moderated greatly since his time in government. 'His idealism is now tempered by the practicalities of administration,' said one Labor man. 'He told me one of the mistakes we made was the commitments we made before we got in in 1972 which prevented us from developing the real priorities.'

Hayden was an early member of Gough's 'kitchen cabinet'—but was dropped a few times when he clashed with the prime minister. According to one top Labor man—who thought Whitlam should have stayed as leader—'Gough liked men who worshipped at the shrine, and Hayden is not that sort'. Eventually, however, Whitlam's and Hayden's paths crossed again and they teamed up in 1975 in a bid to save the Labor government. Whitlam had obviously been impressed by Hayden's working knowledge of economics and his ability to organize. Hayden had been arguing for a long time the need for economic restraint and he finally convinced Whitlam. In fact it is doubtful if any prime minister has praised his treasurer as often as Whitlam lauded Hayden.

In his few months Hayden produced a budget which still leaves its stamp on the tax system, with everyone getting an automatic deduction for medical and other expenses—a system that should have pleased the workers but which certainly upset the insurance companies whose premiums for the most part were no longer a tax deduction.

The man who shared a parliament room with Hayden in Canberra for eight years, Manfred Cross, formerly member for Brisbane, told me once: 'Bill's turning point came when he studied economics. He became a young radical tempered by knowledge and experience.'

One thing is certain about Bill Hayden—he takes his responsibilities as a politician seriously. This taut, fidgety fighter revealed to a friend once while being driven to a conference that he never sleeps the night before a big decision. 'I sometimes envy people who see everything in black and white, left and right,' he said, 'and vote according to that. I never sleep the night before an important decision worrying if it is the right one.'

And no doubt there are others who are now losing sleep wondering if the next prime minister will be an ex Queensland cop.

MYE—WHAT A MAN

There is a Queensland leader in the Torres Strait who is big enough to look Malcolm Fraser in the eye while standing in his bare feet, and whose ability to speak is at Gough Whitlam's level. The Islander is George Mye, chairman of all the eastern islands and a direct descendant of headhunting warriors.

When I heard him address Fraser during the prime minister's tour of the Strait in November 1977 and speak on behalf of the Islanders with his cultured accent and dominating air I wondered which Sydney or Melbourne public school he had attended. Incredibly Mye never left his own tiny island, Darnley, the most remote island within Australian waters. More than thirty years ago, when the junior public examination was the major scholastic goal of educated, white Queenslanders, George Mye passed the exam on Darnley Island. He loved his teacher, Charles Turner, so much that the Islanders brought Turner back to open a home their new housing co-operative had just built.

'We are able to do things ourselves and negotiate with prime ministers, because Mr Turner taught us so well,' Mye told me.

The prime minister was clearly impressed with Mye's proud and articulate manner of address, his creaseless sarong attire, and the two formed an unofficial bond of respect ... like ancient warriors wary of the agility of the other.

Fraser had come to explain to the Islanders why his government wanted to alter Australia's border with the newly independent Papua New Guinea. The border ran right to the mud flats of New Guinea—and the Papua New Guineans, now that they were independent of Australia, wanted it moved halfway between the two countries, cutting the Torres Strait area in two.

When Fraser explained to a meeting of sixty Island leaders that the waters were technically considered international, Mye replied: 'Sir, what you call international waters are to us highways from one island to another.'

He told Fraser that he was very pleased he had come as the first prime minister to visit the Strait: 'We are not people outside on the verandah or underneath the floor waiting to be called,' he said.

And when the prime minister spoke of his new boundary as merely a boundary on the floor of the sea so that Papua New Guinea could have what was under the sea floor while the Islanders roamed the surface, George Mye replied: 'But sir, we are afraid the line will rise to the surface to be a line on the sea, a line on the sky. People must be on top of the sea to get at what is beneath the sea.'

When the prime minister said, somewhat patronizingly, that it was a line the Islanders would not see—'your boats will not run into it, it will be invisible'—this giant black man opened his lips slowly and said: 'Then you had better not tell us it is there, sir.'

He spoke of the Torres Strait as a big pool for Islanders and said that 'even the winds and the tides are ours'. And then, as if to emphasize his effective invective, added: 'We have no scholars to argue for us, only our feelings.'

A man of warrior chieftain proportions, George Mye looks much younger than his forty-nine years, and is a master of subtle politics. Nowhere did Fraser receive such a reception as in the eastern islands. And there to dance for him just happened to be a score of friendly Papuans from the mainland—an indication that the coastal Papuans accept the tradition of separate Australian Islanders.

Fraser saw a dramatization involving the adoration and anointing of a rock symbolizing the creation by Islanders years ago of Bramble Cay—a cay which would be the first thing to go in any lowering of the border. Mye's symbolism did not go unnoticed by government officials who shifted in their seats as these ancient non-Christian rites were used as powerful, though unspoken, arguments against the new border proposals.

Mye became the focal point in the Strait in the battle between the Commonwealth and the Queensland governments for ascendancy, a fight which was particularly worrying for Islanders. They have received many material benefits from both governments and therefore wanted desperately to keep both Bjelke-Petersen and Fraser on side, while at the same time trying to ensure their future within Australia.

Mye's islands have received a lot of Federal funds since 1973—of the order of $700,000—because he started a housing cooperative and other ventures. He was able to show Fraser three very nice homes they had built and workshops—although Queensland let it be known before Fraser left Canberra that these homes had cost $70,000 each. Federal officials acknowledged there were problems, but were also pleased the Islanders were doing something for themselves.

That is why Mye was very shrewd when he presented Fraser with a plate painted by an Islander, a turtle polished and stuffed beautifully by an Islander, and a woven Island handbag for his wife.

Mye said the state government was critical of him because he refused to follow their line. He openly claimed the anti-federal speeches of some other Island leaders had been written by state officials.

'I have a tongue and so I need no one else to speak for me. I welcome very much the efforts the premier has made and that is as much as I want. Because I build houses the state says: "George Mye is going Commonwealth" and I am branded as being the man who is going to give the Strait away.'

Mye said other Islanders were afraid to buck the state government because the state controlled all shipments of stores and all communications.

'They wouldn't let the Island councillors meet here so they could see the houses. The state store here won't cash our cooperative cheques. And when we ordered gas cylinders for cooking for the prime minister they didn't arrive in time.'

The state, on the other hand, said Mye's co-operative was being funded to split the Islanders so the border could be changed. The feds retorted that by exercising an almost total monopoly over communication, supplies and services to the islands the Queensland government was able to maintain the Islanders in a continuing state of dependence.

Which was true. But it was also true to say the state stance on the border was the Islander stance, and that Bjelke-Petersen's truculence helped stop a full border midway between the two countries.

The agreement finally reached in 1978 was very complex but in effect Queensland's border stayed where it was, and all of the Torres Strait Islands—including George Mye's—are still part of Australia.

LABORING WITH BRISBANE

No doubt many Australians would be surprised to learn that the longest-serving Labor government in Australia is voted in safely every three years by nearly half a million people in Bjelke-Petersen's Queensland. It is a Labor government that has survived with the backing of Queensland's voters through the years of Menzies, Holt, Gorton, McMahon and even Fraser.

The government I am talking about is the one which runs Brisbane—and it is one of the most powerful governments in the country. In all, there are eight major governments in Australia and the Brisbane City Council ranks—in terms of voters and budget—a close seventh behind the federal government and five states. It is ahead of Tasmania. As Gough Whitlam said when he was prime minister: 'It has a budget bigger than one state and almost as big as another.'

Unlike other Australian cities, Brisbane is run by a parliamentary style council with enormous powers including control of transport and, until recently, electricity.

The Labor administration in Brisbane though is anything but left wing. Rather it shows more of what the Neville Wran administration has shown in New South Wales—that if a Labor government is prepared to look, act and, eventually, think more like a party of the centre, rather than the right or left, it can be very successful. For it is difficult to imagine a government more removed from the ideas of Tom Uren, Rex Connor or Jim Cairns than the Labor government of Brisbane.

Clem Jones, who led Labor into office and kept them there until he stepped down a few years ago, was a stalwart champion of private enterprise. That is not to say that Clem Jones was not a good lord mayor of Brisbane. His supporters—which included most of the population—loved him. But Jones was pro-freeway, pro-high rise, pro-'development' and anti-public transport. His Labor council turned Brisbane from a town into a city, by seeing that big companies built tall, inner city buildings and giant suburban shopping centres. And in the late 1960s his council destroyed the old tram system which had characterized the city for half a century.

The tram network spanned the city providing noiseless, pollution-free, cheap, and frequent transport. Best of all, the system was totally reliable. The big, open-sided trams suited the hot climate infinitely more than the buses that replaced them. The Labor council bitumined over the tracks and dumped the trams because they were in the way of the motor car.

Of course it is true that at that time it was fashionable to do away with the petrol-free trams which would be such a boon today. Tokyo did the same, though the governor of Tokyo admitted three years ago that it was his greatest error. Some time ago in the U.S. it was revealed that one American city which eliminated its trams did so as the result of offers of city loans from a large oil company, a large tyre manufacturer and a large car manufacturer.

In Brisbane the elimination of trams and introduction of hot, polluting buses forced people with any money at all into buying cars, sometimes two or three to a family. As a schoolboy I travelled all over Brisbane by tram to play football, cricket and tennis. Now mothers driver their children because it is the only way they will ever make it. Salisbury to Clayfield on the one tram ride sounds like a dream today. But the trams were not the only ride the Brisbane people were taken for.

One would expect a Liberal government—dedicated to free enterprise—to allow big companies to rezone residential land for shopping centres (thus immediately increasing the value six or seven times); to hand over parks for sporting clubs to fence them off and clear the trees until all that remains is cleared grass between goal posts. But these things became a Brisbane City Council speciality.

Take, for example, the Labor council's support for the exclusive Indooroopilly Golf Course. Nearby, on a beautiful stretch of the Brisbane River bank, is another eighteen-hole golf course which is on council land but which the council allows the Indooroopilly club to run as a public course. Next to that again is a long pocket of land surrounded by the river which was resumed in 1949 and named the Sir John Chandler Park, after a non-Labor lord mayor. Amazingly, the ALP city council has given this park to the Indooroopilly Golf Club to build a twenty-seven-hole golf course, in return for which the council gets the smaller, developed private course.

The only way this could be justified in the public interest would be if the present developed course were turned into a park with bicycle tracks, horse tracks (as in the London parks), children's playgrounds and tennis courts. (The council obviously hasn't heard about the tennis boom.) And just one golf course takes up the same land as two thousand tennis courts. Instead, the Indooroopilly course will be left as a golf course—so that there will be three-and-a-half almost adjoining courses in the one Brisbane suburb.

When I approached the responsible ALP alderman a few years ago after this plan was announced, he informed me that more golf courses was council policy and that I obviously did not realize the overseas boom. There were 8,000 golfers in Brisbane and, anyway, the courses were park-like open space, he said. Which means that for the other 842,000 non-golfers in Brisbane these wonderful open spaces are about as usable as a rifle range.

The present lord mayor, Frank Sleeman, in three years has created a Bjelke-Petersen-like image of a tough, earthy politician, doing his best for the people. But his Labor administration is slowly overseeing, in my opinion, the death of Brisbane as a potential tourist city by openly encouraging the destruction of the traditional Queensland timber house with galvanized iron roof, set up on stumps. (Not that the Liberal opposition would be likely to stop it either if they won power.)

Brisbane is the only capital city in the world in which white Europeans have grown up in these unique tropical shelters with their wide, cool verandahs, their vertical tongue-and-groove interior walls, their wide horizontal overlapping external chamferboards and their black wooden stumps—keeping the houses as much as possible above snakes, floods, and various other threats. The stumps all wear metal hats so the white ants can't travel up and eat the house. Upwardly mobile white ants are so adept at this (surreptitiously making their entry inside a mud tunnel) that anyone who has been seeing your girlfriend or wife on the side in Queensland is condemned, not as a cad or a bounder, but as a 'whiteanter'. Stumps also enabled houses to be built on hilly ground in the days when excavation was done by shovel—and underneath is a cool place to sit on long summer days, and a good weatherproof storage area.

And the tin roof, it was perhaps the most characteristic element of all. For there is no snugger place in the world in a tropical downpour than beneath a tin roof as the heavy drops drum out a soothing rhythm.

Brisbane could be offered to overseas visitors as the New Orleans of Australia—that is if the council leaves any of these old houses for the tourist to see. One council ordinance rules that if you are on less than sixteen perches (four hundred square metres), as many old homes are near the inner city, you cannot replace you home if it burns down—a big business ordinance which, incongruously, the Liberals have condemned. There must be a way to save most of the remaining Queensland houses which will become, more and more, things of architectural wonder in the future. One way to preserve them would be to allow them to be moved more readily. And the council should not actively encourage the continued building of the square brick boxes which have spilled across Brisbane like red ink in the past decade—earning the title 'the Aspley fortress' after one suburb which is made up entirely of these houses. In many of these areas the only vertical lines in the entire suburb are provided by the unromantic clothes hoists.

Not that this is all the council's fault. Brisbane people in the 1950s lived in wooden or fibro buildings and dreamt of one day getting a brick home, the way people of that era longed to get rid of their old cedar and maple and silky oak furniture for the spanking new plywood numbers. Now many have got their wish, and Brisbane has lost much of its character. It may even be too late to save what remains.

Especially when the Brisbane City Council passes ordinances like this: 'Consent or approval should not be given to erect a building which is a) not of pleasing appearance; or b) has any elevation to street frontage sheeted with corrugated galvanized iron'. Other councils around Brisbane have banned corrugated iron roofs altogether—and people trying to save old Queensland houses from demolition in the city either cannot move them out, or must put a prosaic brick wall under the front verandah.

Probably it happens because the people who enter politics are, by definition, those who hang around the party room for years handing out how-to-vote cards to people who already know how to vote. They do not, with some exceptions, travel widely and thus cannot appreciate the unique beauty of Brisbane. I had to live for seven years overseas before I could see it.

It is a sad fact of life that things are rarely appreciated until they have gone—and so, I fear, it will be when one day there are no more tin roofs and timber houses on stumps in Brisbane. Perhaps they will keep one street intact—just for the tourists.

A LITTLE XENOPHOBIA

SET YOUR CLOCKS BACK ...

The secret of why Queensland will not join the other states in daylight saving has at last been revealed. It is now official that it all has to do with insects getting in cups of tea, dew on the sugar cane, and R certificate movies.

A ten-thousand-word report prepared for the Queensland government recommended that Queensland should not adopt daylight saving. It was prepared by a government-appointed committee of three: C.B. Peter Bell, a former president of the United Graziers' Association, Mrs J. Wilson, past president of the National Council of Women, and A. J. Stratigos, former Queensland manager of the Ford Motor Company.

Listing submissions on 'the disadvantages and inconvenience avoided by Queensland not adopting daylight saving', the committee said a trial period of daylight saving some years ago in the state had forced theatres to show 'a higher proportion of R films' to attract the younger, non-family audience.

It said rural people in Queensland were against daylight saving: 'So much of rural production is tied unbreakably to "sun" time. The harvesting of wheat is governed by moisture content and cannot be advanced by the clock. Dew on sugar cane affects the percentage of extraneous matter and thus involves penalties. The burning of cane is tied to dusk irrespective of the clock to utilize the short period of equilibrium between land and sea breezes. Dairy production falls if cows are yarded in the hotter part of the day. And lettuce can only be planted in the late afternoon.'

As if that were not enough reason to throw the whole east coast of Australia into confusion, submissions were received from organizations in Brisbane, Mt Larcom, North Ipswich, Pleystowe, Tara and White Rock complaining that daylight saving caused 'the loss of one hour's sleep'. The logic of that can only be compared with the lady—who didn't get into this report—who complained that the extra hour of sunlight in daylight saving was peeling the paint on her verandah.

The report went on to show that southern interest in altering Queensland clocks was designed—like some subversive plot—to disrupt the whole fabric of the state's social life. There was 'the added discomfort of needing to dress for dinner'; 'less time spent together as a family'; 'the loss of an extra hour for home to cool before bedtime'; and 'menfolk in rural areas missed radio and TV news services and market reports'. There was the effect on the children: 'children in north Queensland board morning buses in the dark in the wet season months'; 'schoolchildren suffer mental and physical depression and therefore education is sacrificed due to their inability to absorb their school work'; 'children coming home from school exhausted, soaked in perspiration through having to push bikes several miles over rough roads in the heat of summer'.

Not to mention the housewife: 'The washing up doesn't get done until 9 p.m. by the clock', instanced a Wandoan submission.

But anyone doubting that the one hour could make a great difference to children cycling home from school should remember that noon in eastern Australia is in fact not noon in most places—even without daylight saving. 'As Eastern Standard Time is fixed in relation to 150 degrees longitude, noon thus occurs in Mt Isa at 12.48 a.m. EST,' said the committee. 'Thus school buses leaving at 3 p.m. Daylight Saving Time (DST) would leave in Mt Isa at 1.17 p.m. true local time (TLT).'

The committee added that none of the major overseas countries adopting summer daylight saving were within the tropics. Arguments that it worked well in Britain did not apply here. 'The United Kingdom would, if in a southern latitude equivalent to its northern latitude, be wholly south of Tasmania.'

Some business organizations suggested separate time zones within the state—six overall—and one idea was for Queensland to decrease the time difference to half an hour, thus putting everything out of step with everything.

The committee found few real advantages for Queenslanders in daylight saving, though one point taken into account was 'the opportunity to enjoy tea without annoying insects'.

But I'm sure the insects wouldn't really be inconvenienced at all.

STORY OF A BRIDGE

When I was a child at school and the teacher asked me what God made I missed the correct answer 'the world' and replied 'the Story Bridge'. Such is the impact on Brisbane citizens of this towering structure. Like a giant cobweb of steel, the Story Bridge arcs high over the inner city of Brisbane—a monument to what was possible half a century ago. It stands second only to Sydney Harbour Bridge in Australia—but is still the largest bridge designed and built by Australians. It may lack the clean lines of the Hobart and Perth bridges but it dominates the skyline with its complex cantilevered construction.

What really adds to the fascination of the Story Bridge is that it was not only designed by a Queenslander, but also was built by locals working for two Queensland firms which combined to construct it. The Sydney Harbour Bridge, on the other hand, was designed in London and the steel parts were made in Yorkshire and shipped to Australia.

The Story Bridge was designed by Dr John Job Crew Bradfield, who was born at Sandgate in 1867 and who had worked as chief engineer on the construction of the Sydney Harbour Bridge. His knowledge of the Brisbane area influenced him to design the bridge as he did. That's why he wasn't after clean lines: 'The tree-clad hills encircling the city indicated that the cantilever type of bridge, with its lofty towers and powerful river arms, would best harmonize with the picturesque and rugged beauty of the Brisbane skyline,' Bradfield wrote at the time. 'A cantilever bridge, with its plated angles, its bold towers and broad shoulders, whether viewed nearby or afar off will express simplicity, strength and grace.'

Dr Bradfield regarded the building of this bridge, which began on 24 May 1935 and ended five years and forty-two days later, as so important that he produced several volumes of bound books, with photos and drawings, to tell future generations how and why the bridge was built. The bridge at that stage was not named and he called the volumes: 'The Story of King George the Fifth Memorial Bridge ... from Romance to Reality'.

He did not start his story with the discovery of the Brisbane River by John Oxley, as might have been expected: 'At the beginning of time the foundation fabric destined to form the stars, the sun, the planets, this earth of ours, and all the radiation which has been poured out from the sun and the stars ever since, was a chaotic mass of gas, a fire-mist diffused through the whole of space,' Dr Bradfield began. The first photo in the book is not of a bridge but of a cluster of stars—the nebulae M81 in Ursa Major—which he described as 'one of the most beautiful of the star-cities'. Bradfield then jumped forward to the 'Metalliferous epoch' 960 million years ago to explain how the iron ore in Australia was formed—from which the steel for the Story Bridge was made.

Obviously Dr Bradfield felt the Story Bridge would remain as a landmark of human progress, and he was not alone. The premier of Queensland, W. Forgan-Smith, wrote at the time the bridge was built: 'It stands as a monument to the vision, enterprise and engineering prowess of our own people. A Queenslander designed it; a Queensland firm of engineers were the contractors; and Queensland workers built the bridge.'

Moving forward to 400 million years ago, Dr Bradfield wrote that it was probable that a mountain nine thousand metres high (three hundred metres higher than Mount Everest) covered the area where Brisbane now stands. 'The countryside was clad with ancient conifers some of them 150 feet high. The river was a fast-flowing stream with its rock bed much higher and the mouth of the river further east.' A further 100 million years later coal seams formed in swamps in Queensland—the coal used to make the iron ore into steel for the Story Bridge, he explained. Then, according to Bradfield, 220 million years ago showers of white-hot volcanic ash fell over the Brisbane area. 'Where this volcanic ash erupted from no geologist yet ventures to say, but it may be of interest to know that there are several submerged volcanoes, the Tasmantides, about 120 miles off the coast from Southport, the highest being 14,000 feet high.' The white-hot ash set fire to the cedar-like conifers, and when the foundations for the Story Bridge were being dug fossilized tree trunks were found beneath the earth at Petrie Bight among the once white ash.

The coal being used to clinker the cement for the bridge, Dr Bradfield was at pains to explain, came from seams at Dinmore, which formed just 130 million years ago in what was then Lake Walloon—and in one seam were found the imprints of the huge three-toed dinosaurs 'which lived and loved and died in the lake'. And his history of the giant bridge even included drawings of these dinosaurs.

The cement for the bridge was made from coral dredged from Moreton Bay at Mud Island—material that emerged in earth movements about 60 million years ago, and this helped make the Story Bridge unique in quite another way. Concrete is man's artificial stone, and together with steel built the Story Bridge: 'All the materials for the concrete will be obtained from the Brisbane River itself and its estuary. I know of no other bridge in the world where the materials were, or can be, so obtained,' wrote Dr Bradfield.

Shale excavated at Darra near the banks of the river was mixed with the crushed coral. Gravel was excavated from the bed of the Brisbane River near St Lucia to mix with the cement for the concrete. The river gravel was found to make stronger concrete than the blue metal available. It consisted of hard, water-worn pebbles of basalt, diorite and quartz. The river bed also provided 'sharp, hard quartz sand' for the concrete.

But 'steel is man's masterpiece,' wrote Dr Bradfield as he came closer to describing the actual construction, 'the strongest and most reliable material yet manufactured by him.' Engineers have a reputation for being hard-headed pragmatists. But not so this visionary Queenslander. Forgetting about molecular structure and complicated formulae he waxed lyrical and continued: 'Mythology tells us that we owe steel, the most potent factor in the building progress of the world, to the goddess of the Pole Star. This goddess, descending from the starry firmament, became enamoured of a mortal, Siderite, but he, loving none but his brother Sidere, repulsed her. In her wrath she transformed the devoted brothers—Siderite into load stone and Sidere into iron.' He then quoted a poem about iron written in 1707 which concluded:

> One force can draw it from the star above.
> Iron, the symbol of fraternal love.

The iron ore for the Story Bridge was mined at Iron Knob, South Australia, which at the time was the purest haematite ore in the world, with only a one per cent impurity factor.

Up to six hundred men toiled on the bridge, beating it into shape from 55,000 tonnes of cement, 75,000 tonnes of limestone, 20,000 tonnes of steel, and more than twenty kilometres of electric wiring. At the time it was officially rated: 'second in Australia to the Sydney Harbour Bridge and among the most notable in the world'. But while the Sydney Harbour Bridge is bigger overall than the Story Bridge, the Story Bridge is longer and has a wider roadway. The Sydney Harbour Bridge is 1,150 metres long compared to the Story Bridge's 1,345 metres. The main roadway width on the Sydney Harbour Bridge is 17 metres—about a metre narrower than the Story Bridge—but the Story Bridge carries no railway, and the four lines of electric railway in addition to the roadway made the Sydney Harbour Bridge at that time the widest bridge in the world. The total length of the cantilever part of the Story Bridge is 446 metres compared to Sydney's bridge arch of 503 metres. The highest point of the Sydney Harbour Bridge is 134 metres and of the Story Bridge towers, 80 metres.

Because of the complex structure of the connecting steel patterns almost six hundred drawings had to be prepared before work on the Story Bridge started. The successful tenderers were a combination of two firms—Evans-Deakin-Hornibrook Constructions Proprietary Ltd—and records proudly describe these as 'companies of purely Queensland origin both as to capital and management'. All the bridge steelwork was fabricated at the Rocklea, Brisbane, workshops of Evans Deakin, and excavation and concrete work was handled by Hornibrook.

Dr Bradfield designed the bridge with a 282 metre span across the river to give 'an uninterrupted width of waterway for navigation and for the normal flow of the river. Massive piers in the channel would be an obstruction to navigation and to floods,' he wrote. People in Hobart will appreciate what he meant, and so do people in Brisbane as they remember the problems caused by the more modern bridges during the 1974 floods. For anything that slows down a flooded river increases flooding behind it. Dr Bradfield was obviously well aware of Brisbane's major flood potential. He took flooding into account when he decided to build the bridge so high above the river and the city, reasoning: 'The Brisbane River is the principal artery of commerce, linking Queensland with the outside world, and nothing can be done to injure the efficiency and reputation of shipping facilities of the port above the bridge.'

Surveys were done on mast and funnel heights of ships. These were only considered in relation to a high tide because if a major flood were coming the ships would have to get out of the river and might have to leave at full tide. Bradfield decided that steam ships could reasonably be accommodated with a full-tide headway of 30 metres—under the bridge—and concluded that future vessels would have shorter masts. So the Story Bridge has a 30 metre clearance at high tide and 33 metres at low tide.

The steel was manufactured at the Broken Hill Proprietary works, Newcastle, or at Australian Iron and Steel, Port Kembla, and transported to the Rocklea steel fabrication works. More than two hundred workers operated the huge circular steel saws, the giant batteries of hydraulic rivetters, the glowing furnaces and the blinding oxyacetylene jets. 'The gleaming blade of the giant guillotine sliced through inch-thick steel as though it were cheese and mighty overhead cranes swung massive steel girders through the air at 120 feet a minute,' a journalist wrote at the time. In these workshops the men prepared the four main steel bearings for the bridge, each weighing thirty-six tonnes—and on these the entire structure depends. More than one and a quarter million bolts, nuts and rivets were manufactured at Northgate, Brisbane, weighing themselves a total of five hundred tonnes. Workmen splashed thirty thousand litres of paint on and the City Council brought a fleet of diesel buses to carry people across the new toll bridge.

The bridge was built out from both banks towards the middle—ending with the difficult task of joining the structures, high above the river. October 28, 1939, broke calm with light showers and an even temperature—which was very important for this delicate operation. Temperature changes can alter the bridge so dramatically that expansion joints have a movement range of twenty-five centimetres. To take advantage of these ideal conditions taxis went out to awaken the men and they assembled at the bridge at 5 a.m. Thermometers in key places on both sides of the bridge were read and measurements taken. The measurements disclosed differences of only a couple of millimetres between the two sides, and the upper joints closed first after a slight alteration. The bridge was joined without a hitch.

Considering the small volume of traffic at the time of building, the planners showed incredible foresight—for it was estimated that the bridge would, when completed, carry only 8 per cent of the cross river traffic. Yet today, the Main Roads Department's figures show that, even though there are six bridges including the new freeway spanning the river, the Story Bridge now carries an incredible 33 per cent of cross river traffic ... reaching 6,900 vehicles an hour, almost twice the maximum capacity expected. And most of the heavy trucks travel across this huge bridge. When the Story Bridge was closed recently for a bomb hoax traffic came to a complete standstill in central Brisbane.

But the Story Bridge was not only built with an eye to the future. As the Queensland government's own publication to mark the opening on 6 July 1940 said: 'Most importantly it must be remembered that the project was embarked upon at a time of severe unemployment in the metal and engineering trades. The alternative lay between building a bridge which would yield a few per cent return on tolls, or of paying relief to those men, with the certainty of no return whatsoever.

On relief the men's self-reliance and skill would inevitably have deteriorated. After four years' work the state is able to release skilled tradesmen at just the time when Australia needs them most.' For this was wartime.

A third and curiously interesting argument was put forward for building this leviathan—to provide 'uncongested, open-road traffic for health and well-being', because 'the evil effects of city traffic conditions upon health have only lately been realized. Studies of the atmosphere in congested American streets have shown a high percentage of the extremely dangerous gas, carbon monoxide, which can cause severe headaches and digestive disorders. By contrast with these conditions, the Story Bridge offers an open highway.' It is ironic that the Story Bridge now feeds so much traffic through Brisbane's Fortitude Valley that carbon monoxide fumes there are well above the recommended World Health Organization levels.

Perhaps then, in the present period of unemployment in building, architecture and engineering it is time for Queensland to build another bridge—to once again relieve the city of the carbon monoxide threat now facing Fortitude Valley. For Brisbane sorely needs a bridge (or tunnel) between the Story Bridge and the river mouth to connect the industrial southside with the docks and airport on the northside. Even Dr Bradfield was able to foresee forty-five years ago that 'several bridges across or subways under the river may be constructed up or downstream of the Story Bridge'—but he was quick to add, correctly as it turns out, 'but this bridge will always be the most central and most important bridge in Brisbane'.

The bridge was named after John Douglas Story, a longtime Queensland Public Service commissioner who was closely associated with the establishment of Queensland University, and eventually became vice-chancellor. He instigated the state system of classifying public servants. But it should really have been called the Bradfield Bridge.

The souvenir at the opening of the bridge in 1940 proudly announced: 'It stands today a noble and mighty symphony in steel and concrete, a monument of Australian engineering skill, dedicated to the service of those who cross the broad Brisbane River and of the million or more who will one day populate the city of Brisbane.'

It is unlikely that such a feat of local construction could ever be repeated. Many engineers believe that if a giant structure like this were to be considered again it would be designed overseas, with the main parts built there also. For Australians are so used to having their motor cars, their bridges, and their aircraft designed and built by overseas firms that they have forgotten the tale of Queensland's Story Bridge.

GETTING THE PICTURE STRAIGHT

There is a joke that Queensland bananas bend to the right. It's a political joke of course, and it suggests that Queenslanders might be a little twisted. However there's one enterprising young photographer who has confronted this controversial food head-on, and transformed it into an art form.

'I like bananas. I've always liked bananas and I have been photographing them for two years,' photographer Michael Berceanu said as he appraised his photographic exhibition in the Schonell Gallery at Queensland University.

'I didn't want to be the same as everyone else and photograph nude girls ... not that I don't like nude girls. Some photographers are famous for photographing people jumping, others for their pictures of dogs—well I specialize in bananas.'

Berceanu, in his mid-twenties, was born in Brisbane and knows a lot about bananas. He refers to them by their technical names and says he agrees with Queenslanders that Lady Fingers are better eating than Cavendish—the only brand that sells well down south.

It is difficult to judge sometimes just how serious Michael Berceanu is, because of his swift turn of phrase and his constant wry grin.

But his pictures are very serious. His two-week exhibition included big colour pictures of a happy grocer selling bananas, a beautiful phallic-looking banana and a huge bunch of special bananas with a carpet snake curled around them. The photographs were for sale at $100 each.

'I'm now working on a series on just how the banana is treated in our society,' he said. Bananas on a tree, in the markets, in the store, people eating bananas, people playing with them, cooking them and so on.

'There is an immense variety of things a photographer can do with bananas. For instance, I can think literally and use word associations for pictures such as banana bender, banana republic. I'm planning a picture of a dark man in military uniform with bananas instead of epaulettes on his shoulders—and a banana boat.'

Earlier he had been to Southeast Asia to photograph unusual bananas.

'In the Philippines there is even a purple banana and it is one of the great tragedies of my life that I didn't get a picture of one of them,' he said. 'There was none in the markets in Manila so I drove south and hired a canoe to go up a river where they grow along the banks. It took most of the day and by the time I found any it was too dark for photography.'

Berceanu estimates he has taken hundreds of photographs of bananas. 'Bananas are a very talented fruit,' he said. 'They are individually packaged and just the right size for eating when hungry. In the area it takes to grow 40 kilos of wheat you can grow 100 kilos of potatoes but 4,000 kilos of bananas.'

Is there a limit to what can be done with bananas—from an artistic point of view? Mr Berceanu did say he would like to get a picture of Premier Bjelke-Petersen eating a banana. But not everything is possible.

For the future then?

'I already have my next subject lined up—something no one else has even thought of,' he said. 'Papaws. They're beautiful fruit, a lovely shape and ...'

WALTZING OUT OF STEP WITH THE WORLD

One of the nice things about living in Queensland is that often one can, as it were, see Australia from the outside looking in. Thus it is very interesting watching Australia have referendums over what should be the national anthem.

In my seven years abroad writing articles from such diverse places as China, Vietnam, Indonesia and Russia I found that the average person knew two things about Australia—kangaroos and 'Waltzing Matilda'. Yet at home they keep trying to decided between the national anthem of another nation—'God Save the Queen'—and a depressingly chauvinistic and banal song entitled 'Advance Australia Fair'. As the French and Germans know, national anthems are not created, or voted for, they just happen. And it is not something any nation can have two of. Except Australia.

Well Australia got its national anthem decades ago—not at any referendum or dodgy public opinion poll, but conferred upon the country by the world.

After I had lived in England for two years I arrived in Singapore and was walking through the Change Alley market place when a Chinese tailor stopped me and said: 'Say Aussie, you want to buy Waltzing Matilda suit?' Despite my English clothes and haircut and the fact that I hadn't said a word he picked me as they do all the Aussies—by the wrinkles around the eyes.

In Danang in northern South Vietnam at the height of the war the American marines made me sing 'Waltzing Matilda' wherever I went. Invariably they knew the tune, some of the words, and nothing else about Australia. But I noticed they practically stood to attention during my two-verse rendition.

'Mighty fine song,' they would say, 'Aussie.'

Even in China the jolly swagman was just as well known. In Canton in 1965 and in Peking students hummed the tune of 'Waltzing Matilda' and I endeavoured to teach them the words. And that was nearly a decade before Australia even formally recognized the existence of their nation.

When I lived in London the big pirate radio station—Radio London—had an Australian disc-jockey as its breakfast show compere, broadcasting to an estimated audience of eight million. And the programme's theme music was 'Waltzing Matilda'.

In Wales in 1966 when the Australian rugby union team beat them at their own game at Cardiff Arms Park the crowd of forty-five thousand were so impressed that they sang and hummed—not 'God Save the Queen' or 'Advance Australia Fair'—but, of course, 'Waltzing Matilda'. To them, as to everyone else in the world, it is Australia's national anthem. Unfortunately Australians—sitting at home—do not yet realize this.

It is always sad to see someone with an important possession who fails to appreciate it. And thus it is with us: lucky enough to inherit a fine swaggering anthem—and yet still looking around for others. Perhaps a Queenslander can better appreciate the irony because Banjo Paterson wrote the lyrics to 'Waltzing Matilda' on a western Queensland property near Winton in 1895.

CULTURE GOING CHEAP

When the Sydney Opera House, built for close to $100 million, was opened by Herself in a glittering ceremony, up in Queensland there was another glittering ceremony to open a building costing in the vicinity of $200. The place? Julia Creek, about sixteen hundred kilometres northwest of Brisbane. There were no fireworks or processions or orchestras at Julia Creek. There was a queen, though: Councillor Gladys Cooney, known round about as The Queen of Culture.

Julia Creek's Opera House has something else in common with Sydney's. The locals had a devil of a time getting it up and ready. It was the town's dental clinic, once a four-roomed shack with a verandah. Then the Lions decided the town needed a cultural focal point and the council said they could have the clinic so long as they moved it to a prime site at the Julia Creek Civic Centre (No harbour views there.) The Lions thought they could manage the move for about $50, plus a coat of paint and the demolition of a couple of walls. A couple of months would do it. But, as with opera houses everywhere, costs escalated as time marched on.

'We ran into construction difficulties,' said Bob Marshall, the Lions' secretary. 'We found we were unable to move it in time with volunteers so we had to get a contractor in for $110. Apparently there were difficulties in moving it in anything but one piece because of the design of the corrugated iron roof.' Holding up the roof without interior walls proved to be another problem. Round about then the locals began calling it the Opera House, 'because we're all amateurs and it was taking so long'.

By the time the last coat of paint (cream and royal blue) was put on it, the Julia Creek Opera House had cost $200, more than four times the original estimate. To defray the expense, the town had its own Opera House Lottery. The law being a bit churlish about these unofficial lotteries, the first prize was only a wallet—though what was in it the locals wouldn't say.

So, while Sydney raved on with fireworks and orchestras, Julia Creek turned on with a steak barbecue, a keg or two and a speech or two. While Sydneysiders were togged out in their tails and long dresses, it was open-necked shirts and shorts for the men and slacks for the ladies of Julia Creek, though Councillor Cooney wore a long skirt.

And while the opening concert down south had the Sydney Symphony under van Otterloo, Julia Creek had Burt Bacharach—on record, of course.

SIMPLY NAIVE

Charles Callins is one of the most unlikely painters in Australia. Clean-shaven, short-haired and aged ninety, he never considered painting until he was sixty-three, and then painted his first work with housepaint left over in a cupboard in his old weatherboard home. All of his paintings are done on the front verandah on a table covered, in Queensland fashion, with a piece of kitchen floor lino. In front of him ancient wooden shutters open out onto an incongruous view of the skyscrapers of Brisbane—all concrete and glass—in the valley below his home.

But his paintings are not, as might be expected, painful landscapes of Brisbane scenes, but rather primitive visualizations of his ninety years in Queensland—simple paintings of how he remembers things almost invariably as seen by someone watching from the sky.

'It is as if they are in there in a lump in my mind. I suppose and every now and then one comes out,' he explained.

His paintings appear childlike in composure—but they have a feeling for unusual colour, dominated by exaggerated blues and greens, a different shade in every painting. Many are of the sea and his early life in Cairns and seem to lack any perspective, with no shadows and no thought for comparative sizes of things. 'The perspective is in my own mind and I try to avoid clashing. Shadows would put darkness where I don't want it, colour is important in my paintings,' he says.

Callins is intense in his interests and when I arrived I was ushered in by his eighty-four-year-old wife, Nellie, and he greeted me with the words: 'Don't worry you won't be stuck for a story.' He then proudly produced an exercise book recording his other activity since he retired—'voluntary ("make sure you say voluntary") swimming coach'—with every swimmer's race time faithfully noted. Above one girl's record he had written in red: 'The Golden Girl'.

When he was sixty Callins was advised by his doctor to retire from work and to take up swimming for his injured left leg. His exercise-book history of his coaching recounts that because he did not like swimming in fresh water he returned to Cairns for a few years to swim in the pool there, because it was salt water, and built himself up from nine to eleven stone.

He returned to Brisbane and started swimming in a local pool and helping youngsters to swim. This gave him a new lease of life and one night he came home and told Nellie: 'If I don't paint Green Island [off Cairns] and the Barrier Reef I will die and take the story with me.' He had never had a lesson in painting. 'Never any yearning'. But he felt Green Island was 'absolutely so beautiful it should be painted by someone'.

He was about to become Charles Callins, painter of the naive school, represented in the Australian National collection in Canberra, the Queensland Art Gallery and in private collections around the world ... Princess Anne has one of his paintings and recently in Sydney he was honoured by his third one-man exhibition.

'I was sitting in this house at this table and I had some house paint but I didn't know how far I was going to go. I sketched it quick and lively from my mind and made a box frame and tacked some canvas on it. I knew about colours from job printing and, because I had to wait for certain parts to dry, it took me two weeks. Even then I knew not to waste my time with water paints—all my paintings can go out in the wet.

'I didn't know what to think of it and I took it down to Wynnum Creek and three girl teachers who saw it said to me: "Don't you stop painting".'

In 1954 the queen provided inspiration for Callins. He went to the house next door where he could look across to Government House sitting atop another of Brisbane's thirty-seven hills. 'It took a lot of thinking out. I cut out all the buildings and streets so they wouldn't spoil the painting and shade what I wanted to do. I made it all bushland with the main road a track and drew Government House on the hill. I got a photo of the queen at a surf carnival looking reflective and painted her at the bottom thinking about her two children in a heart at the top. And then I drew the duke with his hand under the queen's chin as if he was asking her "A penny for your thoughts Elizabeth", and that's what I called it.'

This was when Callins decided to continue as a painter, for when he took it down to Ithaca baths (where he was coaching) he was asked if it was a photo. 'That's what made me go further.'

What Callins likes about his paintings is that they tell stories. 'All my big paintings have a story on the back. They have a lot to say—they are not stuck for words.' And he showed me a colour photo of one of his paintings he has been advised never to sell, called 'Accomplished', which tells his life's story since he married Nellie in 1920.

He explains it all on the painting: 'We climbed the highest mountain, we walked the fields and hills, we walked along the beach and sailed the ocean seas. And when we came back—we rested our weary bodies watching budgies, parrots and kookaburras in the trees and we had four children and there they are here.'

This is the reason he doesn't like abstract painting. 'It doesn't explain itself. If you look at a painting I feel it should give you a result. Even colour—a thing that would be red is black or it might be blue or pink, but not red. They don't consider colours, they just slap it on. They don't try to make the painting speak for itself. You shouldn't have to fathom for three hours to know what it is.'

He revealed two vital ingredients in his works: 'I always paint the sky in first ... and colour's important. If it's blue make it blue, that's my idea,' he said.

One interesting thing about his paintings is that while he visualizes them from his mindlife he is almost invariably in the painting himself and he believes that that is the position he is viewing it from. For example in one painting of Green Island and the north Queensland coast which is like a view from a cloud I asked him where he was viewing it from: 'That's me there. I'm in that boat,' he replied.

Two years ago he did a painting of himself aged twenty-six at a ladies impersonation contest which he won in Cairns in 1913. He was on the stage in wig and dress throwing roses which landed, accidentally, in the police commissioner's lap. But the painter was above them all, suspended somewhere in the roof. Callins, though he doesn't see it that way himself, is a birdseye view painter. A remarkable example of his ability to see things from above is illustrated in a painting which took four months to paint and which Callins says was stolen and has disappeared. It is of the Girls' GPS Swimming Carnival in Brisbane as if seen from a helicopter and painstakingly shows row upon row of the thousands of girls around the pool in their respective school uniforms, and girls in lanes stroking up the pool. I could even recognize some schools in the photo of the painting. 'But I took their hats off to make it plainer,' he said.

On lined exercise paper on the desk was the preview of his next painting—a scrawl of red, a scribble of blue and some shaped pencil lines.

'Remember cyclone Ted?' he said. 'Well while it was going on in north Queensland I looked out my bathroom window and that's what I saw two thousand miles away. It was just getting dark—the pencil lines are the buildings. The sky was dark blue above them, but above it there was this strange red reflection, an awful light from end to end of the sky.'

DAM IT ALL

In Queensland when they want to illustrate the size of a project they somehow always end up comparing it to Sydney Harbour. Not that anyone in Queensland is all that impressed by Sydney Harbour, but it is the only way locals know of impressing the purse-string holders in Canberra with the importance of projects.

This time it's a proposed dam that could hold sixteen times more water than Sydney Harbour. The site is on one of Australia's big rivers which many probably have never heard of—the Burdekin, a giant river flowing out of the Great Divide to the coast between Ayr and Home Hill in north Queensland. Since Australians started talking about the possibility of a Snowy Mountains hydro-electric scheme, Queenslanders have been pointing out that the Burdekin has as much, or more, potential for producing cheap power—and at the same time populating the north and fattening half a million cattle a year.

State politicians have been promising since at least 1949 to do something about getting the river dammed to take advantage of the huge volume of water that races downhill and out to sea every year. In 1952 an article in a Queensland paper began: 'What is holding up the building of the Burdekin dam?' The article quoted the commonwealth government as being 'doubtful' about the scheme and the state ALP cabinet as 'enthusiastic'. The same year premier Vince Gair advocated the building of the dam and various announcements have been made in the thirty years since then. In 1968 the then Country Party premier, Jack Pizzey, announced that the scheme was to be re-appraised by Canberra—but nothing ever happened. And again, in mid 1977, when Bjelke-Petersen's cabinet meeting in the northern capital city of Townsville 'approved the Burdekin River hydroelectric scheme', there were dismayed cries. The announcement read like a re-run of an old TV movie. With an election due within six months this decision, at a specially convened cabinet meeting just north of the Burdekin, looked suspiciously like an election ploy. 'The Burdekin: Here We Go Again', said a headline in the Brisbane *Courier-Mail*.

A committee was to be appointed to recommend ways of implementing the scheme: 'I hope construction will be under way in the 1980s,' Bjelke-Petersen said. The Queensland premier said it would need to be a federal-state scheme such as the Snowy Mountains project—which meant the tight-fisted Canberra government would have to agree to part with hundreds of millions of dollars for a scheme to benefit Queensland.

If the dam was built it would provide cheap power to all of north Queensland, but that seems unlikely to influence Canberra—and a project that in 1951 would have cost a mere $70 million now would need to siphon off $500 million or more. And who's going to spend that sort of money on a river they've probably never heard of?

AN INNOCENT QUEENSLANDER ABROAD

MELBOURNE: FOR MONEY AND MIDDLEMEN

Soon after my father was born in Victoria his father took him aside and gave him some good old-fashioned advice: 'Son, when you grow up make sure you get a collar and tie and a coat, as fine a coat as you can afford, and never take them off.' My grandfather, of course, was not advocating that my father never wash. After a hard life in mining towns in the west and north of the country he was telling my father that the easiest role in life was to be a middleman—preferably a Melbourne middleman.

Dad was too young to understand what he meant, and foolishly set off for the frontiers of Western Australia and then Queensland, and never saw a collar and tie until he married. But, having now been to Melbourne, I know what this family story meant.

It is a strange fact that three-quarters of the Australian population is huddled in the tiny southeastern corner in a triangle through Sydney, Canberra, Melbourne, Adelaide—a peninsula covering only 7 per cent of the Australian land mass. And near the centre of this triangle is Melbourne—the city with the closest thing to a European climate that mainland Australia could provide. Here have gathered those shrewd enough to put on their collars and ties and coats and never take them off ... the Australian middlemen—the lawyers, politicians, financiers, bankers, finance company executives, company directors, traders.

Before I went to Melbourne I knew they were there—cliche Collins Street, financial centre of Australia, and all that—but I didn't realize how well they were doing. They buy those lovely old Victorian homes for a small fortune, Porsches proliferate like Holden specials, and the shopping went way beyond my imagination—they obviously send the dregs up to Sydney, and their leftovers to Brisbane.

The trendy place for shopping is Toorak Road—and I don't mind admitting that I gaped in awe. The first thing I noticed was the brown velvet chesterfield lounge suite in the women's shoe shop for the ladies to sit on while trying on their imported Italian shoes at an arcade called The Place. The economy is supposed to be in ruins, but these shops were packed and I couldn't get into the chocolate shop to buy some imported Swiss chocolate.

Then I saw a most amazing thing—frangipani trees as pot-plants for sale at ten dollars each. People in Queensland still won't believe me when I tell them this—you just break a branch off any frangipani tree and stick it in the ground and it grows.

The imitation of the French in a city noted for its waspish clubs and attitudes was a surprise. Taped French music filtered through the arcade (Charles Aznavour) and the small eating place sold imported French soups and served *pâté* on rye. In Melbourne mascara is no longer black, it is *noir*. Of course it is no use having this sort of shopping if there are not the customers to afford it. And Melbourne can afford this because the head offices of the big companies are also huddled as far south as they can get, mostly in Collins Street.

It is stating the obvious to say that the real money ends up at the head office—that if Comalco in north Queensland is doing very well CRA in Collins Street must do even better. The banks and the insurance and finance companies proliferate in Melbourne—in Collins Street I passed four major bank offices in a row. These are the real winners if the Queensland cattleman or wool producer comes good. If he doesn't they coin anyway and own his property.

Everywhere there are reminders of what has happened to Queensland. I passed the head office for Myer—one of the southern stores that moved into Queensland and turned local stores into branch offices in the 1960s. There is the Herald and Weekly Times which controls what is euphemistically called Queensland Press, the owner of Queensland's two major dailies. There is Carlton United which came to Brisbane and took over a local brewery and has just marketed a beer called Brisbane bitter—'the taste you can stay with'. For those up in Queensland, it's been bitter all right. All the big companies, like Ford and Qantas, have extensive public relations set-ups in places like Melbourne—but despite the more than two million people in Queensland they have nothing like that in the north. Qantas, in fact, has always annoyed me because almost all of its flights from Southeast Asia go to Brisbane via Sydney or Melbourne. I know it is only a few thousand kilometres out of the way for Queenslanders, but it is a bit like going to London via Greenland. When I lived in Singapore they did have one flight a week that landed in Brisbane first—at five o'clock Sunday morning. And this from a company that advertises itself in Queensland as 'Qantas, the airline Queensland gave the world'.

Even our federal government comes mostly from Victoria. Six of the twelve inner cabinet members are Victorians, and only one is from Queensland. And it almost goes without saying that there is no cabinet minister from the northern half of Australia.

Melbourne's wealth has led to different lifestyles. I ran into a Queensland journalist who was a tanned, blonde surfie two years ago—now he is pale and dark haired from the good life indoors. Journalists who in London wore cords and desert boots and never had more than five pounds in their pockets are now three-suits-a-year, fifteen-shirts-in-the-wardrobe men and working for large companies. When I asked one for a closer look at a fifty-dollar note, he produced seven from his wallet.

Businessmen are obviously in the money, and it is not all going in taxes as it does with ordinary workers. For there are plenty of sharp accountants in a place like Melbourne. 'Art directors with talent to equal your own,' said the big advertisement, 'and money. The right amount, paid the way you want it.' And the way most would want it would be tax-free.

But at least the city has kept all its lovely old buildings in the central city—and, unlike Brisbane and Sydney, Melbourne has been wise enough to keep its trams. As well as moving thousands of people more efficiently than any other form of transport, the trams give a city an air of togetherness. Melbourne is now calling itself the garden city—and it deserves the accolade. The city has made a lot of the

Yarra and there is a lesson for Brisbane in the way the banks have been turned into parks on the water's edge. Then there is the bicycle track now built along next to the river.

The topography may be flat but the houses with their high fences are very private and the localized city councils—instead of the one huge administrative machine as in Brisbane—take advantage of local pride and keep footpaths, roads and trees shipshape.

Even the political personalities are special. I went to have a look at Bob Hawke, who is smaller than I expected. The local reporters told me he would have a jacket with him but would not put it on for TV interviews—he never does, they said. Part of the image and the accent I guess. And he didn't. He combed his thick head of greying hair, put down his coat but, perhaps mindful of my grandfather's dictum, he kept it close by, and in his raucous voice took what I thought was a very unfriendly line with the press. 'Would you be more specific?' one journalist asked. 'I could be, but I'm not going to be,' he said. Then he took so long to answer a question, talking for minutes without seemingly taking a breath, that reporters rolled their eyes at me in frustration.

Melbourne is certainly an elitish city. I only had to look over the Melbourne Cricket Ground to see that. I never realized the ground was so huge. There I was surrounded by more than a hundred thousand empty seats on three levels—it made the 'Gabba look like a picnic ground. But while the masses sit out on these levels the class of Melbourne have the best view of any cricket ground in the world from the long room—as its name implies, an elongated room with long black leather chairs lined up in front of unobstructed glass windows, with a good view for those standing behind these chairs at the bars. A black printed notice confirmed grandad's turn-o'-the-century advice. It read 'lounge suit or sports attire with jacket and tie or cravat'. That would rule out everyone at the 'Gabba, even the members.

Posh Melbourne is the land of Geelong Grammar which, while I was there, explained in the school quarterly *The Corian* that the school did badly at football because 'it is not really a rich man's sport'.

Perhaps the biggest criticism I can make of Melbourne is that it is snug and smug in its isolation at the bottom tip of the mainland. In world terms it is a little known city. Nothing exemplifies this more than the brand of football the city follows. While New South Wales and Queensland and the rest of the world thrill to soccer and rugby, Melbourne thrills to its own peculiar brand, and despite instant transmissions by TV of international soccer and rugby it still sticks to a football it can never play against anyone else. Some say they follow the game with a dedication no one else can match because in a Melbourne winter there is nothing else to do.

I won't comment much on their football—called aerial pingpong in Queensland—because I don't understand it. But they do have a player I saw on a TV grand final called Jesenko, or something like that, who would have made a reasonably good inside centre. Personally I like the way the fellows in white shorts run out to the centre with girlish strides to give the referee the ball, and the goal umpires who signal like aircraft carrier landing guidance officers. The idea of the game seems to be to try to kick the ball to the biggest bunch of players—and then roll it along the ground toward the opposition goal line ... I think.

Despite this eccentricity, I decided that Melbourne was a European-style haven of sophistication. It was finally brought home to me when I read the following ad for an expensive home in Melbourne: '... With delightful touches like a circular window inset with stained glass kookaburras.'

Real style that.

CUSHY CANBERRA

Parliament House in Canberra resembles a giant Rinso-white boarding school in the centre of an entire city created specially to look after the privileged students.

For the average Queensland politician it is all a bit hard to take—most of them didn't make it to Geelong Grammar. They are not used to running at the ringing of a bell as are old boarding school chaps, and because of this keep missing divisions. They get irate letters from party Whips—the prefects—and in a recent circular the head prefect threatened to tell the headmaster—none other than Prime Minister Malcolm Fraser, to those in the know, or 'Pal Mal' as some call him. In the members' dining room long tables with white tablecloths are lined up as in any private boarding school.

Because of its peculiar location all the members have to leave their homelands and journey to live in Canberra for much of the year. They board at hotels on special cut rates for long stays and commute from their dormitories to sit the day in a giant classroom type atmosphere—of green leather in the House of Representatives—where they listen to their leaders speak, and very occasionally are called upon to speak themselves.

One I know gets so lonely he rings friends in Brisbane daily to find out who was lunching at the Milano and who made it to the Shield cricket at the 'Gabba the day before. For despite the government majority they must attend all divisions so things won't 'look bad'. One disaffected government backbencher sits at his desk, fills the wastepaper basket, reads the papers, joins everyone in the House for question time—the only time it is full—and then hangs around until 11 p.m. just in case there is a division. Naturally this leads to a lot of what Canberra does more of than anywhere else in Australia—drinking. In my week in Canberra I saw more grog flow than in a year in Queensland.

Drinking—in restaurants, in bars and in hotels—is the national capital's pastime. My Canberra motel even puts fourteen dollars' worth of grog in every room, which patrons are automatically charged for—though you can get a refund if you prove you didn't drink it all. Much of the drinking is done in the non-members' bar at Parliament House where journalists and politicians stand around telling each other about 'constituents who bite their members' and reporters who are 'well strung'. Even the shops in Canberra are full of grog. At one tiny shopping centre no fewer than three shops sold grog—row upon row of it like the dog food section at Woolies.

One night in the last week of sittings there were three parties going at once along the labyrinthine corridors of the maze that is our Parliament House. One was for the Liberals elected in 1975—immediately labelled 'the oncers show' by a cynic because many of them were likely to lose at the 1977 election. From the front verandah in Tony Street's office at 1 a.m. I drank scotch and wondered what the poor people were doing, what time the Queensland graziers and cane farmers would be up in the morning to beat the heat to dip their cattle for ticks, or to harvest the cane. Below me I could see rows of government drivers, on overtime, standing in groups near their big white limousines chatting and looking up at the party.

I left and visited some friends and found that at 2 a.m. it was absolutely impossible to get a taxi in Canberra. I couldn't even get the company on the phone. At 2.30 a.m. I did and the man apologized. 'We are very busy taking calls from Parliament House,' he told me.

In Canberra, you see, Parliament House gets all the taxis at certain times and then ordinary people just have to wait. It was like that when I arrived at the airport. I got in a long queue for a taxi—and noticed that all the taxis as well as big white Fords were pulling up further down the track to pick up other people. I slipped inside and found a score of people at a desk labelled 'government cars': a service specially for public servants.

Fifteen minutes later I shared a cab with three businessmen. 'Don't worry, I will take you fellas,' the driver said. 'All the other cabs are taking the calls for the shiny arses but I won't be in it for the shinies. They would leave you here for ever, they have got to look after the clowns first and the workers next.' I thanked him for his consideration.

I got him to take me for a drive, during which he described the federal capital to me. 'I would just like to see a bit of untidiness, an advertising billboard, some peeling paint,' he gasped. 'Even a dog run across the road. And I would like to be able to stop at a corner store for a headache powder but there aren't any.' And he was right. In Canberra advertising hoardings are banned, so apparently are potholes and untidiness.

'You see that piece of paper over there,' the driver said, 'that'll be gone by the time we get back, some fella with a spike on a stick will pick it up. You can bet on it.'

He had come to Canberra when he saw the trees and parks and now regretted it. Apparently the cast-iron soul of the public service, the esoteric iron-lung isolation from the real Australia was getting to him.

'They should put a fence around it and call it a cemetery,' he said. 'See that lawn—that will be mowed today and the sprinklers will come on. The people here sit and watch the problems of the rest of Australia on TV and say "fancy that" and that's it.'

The taxi driver took me out to the isolated outskirts of Canberra where everything is quiet and orderly and the shops are kept in small groupings away from roads.

'The women out here who don't work tell me they can hear the grass growing and it is driving them mad. There is a sadness about this city.'

He was worried about bringing his children up there. 'It is unrelated to any other part of Australia. Truck drivers arrive pushing their sleeves up and laughing at the shiny arses and three months later they are on a bus in a uniform, and the next step up is to drive the LTDs for the politicians and civil servants, and they get collar and tie and they think they have made it. Promotion is so quick in the public service that within six months a youth can be a class seven and the sevens want to be eights, and the eights nines, and so it goes on. I went on a job to pick up an eighteen-year-old the other day and he turned up his nose and said "I'm expecting a white LTD." It's a bit hard to take, mate. And what about my kids. When I took them to my home town of Goulburn my son described the oval as terrible. "It wasn't even mowed," he said. But how can I expect them to relate to the rest of Australia when there is not another bloody place like this in Australia.'

The driver showed me how the only service stations were in the isolated shopping nests, which he said were all the same. 'The whole place is the same. I find when I drive around the sameness fossilizes my mind. Every suburb is the same—I can't tell the difference. I'd be lost if you turned me around twice.'

I soon learned that the only way to catch taxis was to ring up. My first few attempts at going for a walk to get one taught me several things about Canberra—nobody walks, despite the provision of elegant footpaths; taxis therefore don't cruise; and the wide roads, which would be classed as freeways if they existed in Queensland, are difficult to cross safely.

Canberra, in fact, is beautiful but out of date. Like Los Angeles it was built for motorists. The city even has an un-Australian climate—a continental climate with a hot summer and a cold winter when people go to the snow fields and trout fishing. Its colonnaded shops are more reminiscent of New Delhi or Singapore than Australia. The only thing Australian about Canberra is the gum trees.

In many ways it is like Louis XVI's court at Versailles—a planned palace for the rulers to spend their lives unadulterated by the working classes. It is a thicket of advisers, academics, economists and public servants who have found the ideal setting for theory, a nest removed from the normal range of occupations and problems, a city insulated from adversity. It is the seat of government where politicians are desperately trying to peg back inflation—but if they got up one morning and looked around they would see that if the rest of the country were to be given the facilities of Canberra, Australia would be broke before lunchtime.

The roads resemble black silk ribbon flattened by a steam iron.

While an important northern city like Mount Isa still doesn't have an all-bitumen road to the coast, I crossed Canberra from one edge to the other—thirty-three kilometres—and without breaking the speed limit, in half an hour. It is absurd, too, that a city of only two hundred thousand should have sprawled so far across—farther than Brisbane—but of course they had to make room for the artificial lakes and the parks. And while Pal Mal and his boys talk austerity, Canberra, with the best roads in the world, is pushing ahead with a $20 million freeway, called the Molonglo—$20 million for just a few kilometres of mercury-smooth Canberra road.

In Parliament itself the members jump up and down in front of the Speaker in his ridiculous wig and gown. From the press gallery they resemble schoolboys shaking their hands in the air and calling 'please sir'. The backbenchers—looking bored and almost lying down in their chairs—are there purely as numbers and they tell me they are not supposed to ask questions without clearing them with the relevant minister. That's democracy. In the centre, Fraser and Hayden sit opposite each other across a narrow table, in what must be uncomfortably close proximity.

Mostly the MPs are not speaking for each other, for the seven or eight in the public gallery or for the few friends in the stalls—they are speaking for the press gallery, hoping to get some media coverage.

Canberra is a difficult city to miss from the air, it is the green bit in the middle of a typically brown Australian landscape—as if to symbolize to arrivals its policy of keeping the lush life for Canberra, and leaving the rest of the country out in the drought.

The biggest problem for the inhabitants then is not recession or drought, inflation or flood—for the city is insulated from all that—but where to find a car park two minutes from the office.

Canberra is an artificial city, a public service city that is wealthy, affluent and complacent. It is a city of moneyed gentry, akin to titled aristocracy. There are no workers, no one producing anything they can point to, except perhaps bundles of paper. It is as if they all exist to take in each other's washing, for the people of Canberra feed off the country and live off the public service—the car driver, the bus driver, the garbageman, the motel bed makers, the carpenters.

It is a pity, I believe, that Canberra exists. It should have been put in Sydney or Melbourne where it would have been just another function of a big city. In Canberra government IS the city. Those sole judges of truth who now live in Canberra would have lived and seen Australians as they are—not as they would like them to be.

But Canberra has been there too long for us to expect to see things change. In fact so long that what worries me is that our leaders of the future will come from a whole new race of people born and bred in Canberra. And as Tennyson would have added: 'That hoard, and sleep, and feed, and know not me.'

SEX AND SIN IN SYDNEY

The first thing I did in the big smoke of Sydney was to drop my ports off on the duchess in the hotel room, buy a *Playboy*, and head for Kings Cross looking for a slice of southern action. Being from Queensland I knew I would have to be careful—our reputation for barbaric corruption and repressive, malevolent government could get me into real trouble in this democratic haven of honesty. No short-back-and-sides, no drawl, no naive remarks, no dung on my jackboots. Ready.

'You from Queensland,' said the astute taxi driver. Before I could issue a denial he said he picked the deep north background by the *Playboy* under my arm. That's the trouble with a free society. He even knew *Playboy* had been banned in Queensland since 1964.

'Throw it away. I will show you some shops that make it obsolete,' he told me.

As luck would have it this taxi driver also knew the location of several illegal casinos—the ones the Sydney police have been unable to find for a decade. He took me to one at Kings Cross—I picked it because of all the drawn blinds—and he wouldn't take any extra money from me for the risk he had taken in this clandestine, illegal act. But then he was fairly flush anyway because one of the two men guarding the entrance owed him some money and gave him ten dollars when he introduced me.

As I went up the long narrow staircase the two men slumped back into their chairs just inside the entrance way. They looked very sullen but were probably tired as they had been doing their Christmas shopping—I could tell from the way their pockets bulged.

The casino—the palace they call it—was very big with a dozen separate tables and, I was glad to see, even a chocolate wheel. A couple of hundred Sydneysiders gathered around long green tables, eyes fastened on either girls in long black gowns dealing cards or men encased by the respectability of dinner suits spinning ivory balls around the large varnished wheels set into tables. To add a touch of Sydney's obvious class there were plenty of plastic chandeliers and red velvet wallpaper and the croupiers did away with all that French talk they use in overseas casinos and called things like 'no more bets' and 'stop'. It wasn't at all the temporary structure I had expected: so that it could quickly be turned into a bridge club at a moment's notice as in the American movies. But I bet they had some such ingenious system in case of a raid.

The chief croupiers sitting in high chairs looked quite fierce and, being from a state renowned for its corruption, I began to worry that I might be recognized. For a moment I thought the manager had picked me in one for, with surprising agility for a big fat man held in by a white belt, he leapt across at me as if to play a forehand return and started subdued shouting. My mind was racing: perhaps it was the telltale skin cancer indentation above my right eyebrow that gave the game away? Or the tanned face? I knew I shouldn't have worn riding boots. Thank God I wasn't still carrying *Playboy*.

But it was OK. Calm down, I thought, the taxi driver didn't say anything. How could he know I was from a police state? All he wanted to do was to ask me to quieten down—I had struck up a conversation with a nice fellow who wanted to invite me home to see some slides. But I hate slide nights. Apparently this manager can't stand loud noise or talking. He doesn't like sunlight either, because not only were the curtains drawn but they were taped and pinned shut, even around the exhaust fan. It seemed such a waste of daylight saving to me. I mean, if you are going to go to all the trouble of changing the time ...

After this initial shock I sauntered across to the bar as if nothing had happened and ordered a quiet stiffener. For foreigners like me the drinks were very expensive, because I handed a ten dollar note to the girl in the plunging neckline and never got any change. In fact she wouldn't even look at me again. But I did notice that locals all came up and got their drinks for free.

So old fatso wasn't such a bad guy after all: free drinks for the locals who play his casino, despite the high overheads he kept complaining about—a nice gesture, although I wouldn't like to be gambling with those blue hundred-dollar chips with too many under my belt. But in a state with modern attitudes like New South Wales I suppose just about everyone can hold a lot of liquor, which is so important if you are gambling. You wouldn't want to lose your better judgment.

Despite the liquor and the gambling nobody seemed very happy. They sat or stood grim-faced watching their own personal wheel of fortune, not even reacting when they won. One bloke I felt particularly sorry for kept pulling bundles of fifty-dollar bills from his pocket, changing them into chips, then losing. Each time he would say to the blonde, his wife I guessed, behind him: "There's another thousand dollars gone," and she would squeeze his hand and he would have another free drink. They really are modern in Sydney too, because his curvaceous wife didn't go home with him when he ran out of rolls—she stayed on and, in fact, I saw her holding another player's hand. And he wasn't winning either.

One charming chap tried to reassure me about the police and said there would be no raid. No chance, he said. But I still felt disquiet. I mean, coming from a state ruled by such a tyrannical, despotic government probably clouded my judgment, but I felt sure that out there was one honest policeman who, come what may, would march past those two men at the bottom of the stairs, defy all corrupt officials, and walk in and announce: 'You are all under arrest. Casinos are illegal.' On the basis of numerical probability, when you get a state with several thousand policemen there has got to be one, there is always one—look at Whitrod in Queensland—who will do the wrong thing. I could almost hear him coming up the stairs. Any moment this handsome man in blue, with blonde hair and observant gaze, would park outside and step into the room to do his duty. But I kept imagining him without a gun on his hip—we find that unnecessary, if not downright distasteful in Queensland.

My friend wouldn't have any of it. 'Look,' he said, 'calm down. If there are any honest cops they put them on the day shift.'

'Yea,' said his friend, 'or they send them out to Wagga Wagga.

That's the trouble with youse Queenslanders, you are too used to tyranny.'

But being born and bred in Queensland I couldn't get that honest cop off my mind so I left by the stairs to seek out sex and sin in Kings Cross.

There wasn't much obvious sin. There were a lot of very nice ladies for such a shady area who kept inquiring after my health and wanting to know if I was lonely—they must have known I was down from Queensland. I had to wait until they weren't looking to slip into an adult sex shop which was lit up like a Christmas tree. Its customers obviously had a lot of class and a sign in the entrance said: 'Kindly finish food, drink and ice cream before entering.' That taxi driver was so right about *Playboy*. This shop had everything—animal as well as human—but I wasn't really impressed. 'No, we don't have *Playboy*,' the rather nasty man behind the counter told me with a look of disgust. Anyway I wanted to get out before that conscientious policeman arrived. Not that I should have worried. Even the banks were in on it—you could use Bankcard at the sex shop.

Wanting to see still more of this tolerant society, the mecca for Australians, I again overlooked the Opera House and the bridge and caught a taxi to a leagues club.

Pulling the handles on those machines must be a heck of a lot of fun. In a big carpeted room there stood four hundred poker machines and at each one a couple of people gathered and fed coins with a rapidity that left little room for working out the odds for a jackpot. But then I was probably just showing my ignorance again. I mean they wouldn't be putting all that money into a machine unless it was giving more money back, would they?

I was told that the club nets something like twenty thousand dollars a week from the machines—and the New South Wales government, though it doesn't balance its books as Queensland does, gets a lot closer because of tax on these machines.

The friendly atmosphere of the club was no doubt reinforced by the surveillance cameras and no less than nine men circulating to watch for cheats—looking over shoulders. Not that, I am sure, this sort of thing encourages the criminal element, but security men did tell me that the poor American company that sells all these machines now has to charge twice as much because so many anti-theft devices are needed. Despite the cameras and security men thefts using electric drills still take place.

I liked the way the pokies rang bells when they paid out—it sounded so exciting and urged everyone to keep trying—but it also enabled the ever-vigilant guards to watch for too many payouts from a particular machine. Anyway it was a comforting feeling to know there were so many people guarding me and cameras keeping an eye on me and even a microphone so that even if I just whispered for help, should I need it, the monitor man would hear me. There's nothing like democracy to give a place a club atmosphere.

I was told that Queensland rugby league clubs were all set to go 'pokie' a couple of years ago and the American machines were actually loaded on trucks covered with tarpaulins—but that ogre Johannes Bjelke-Petersen just wouldn't come across no matter what persuasive arguments were put up. That's the trouble with having a despot for a leader. One of his staff even had a look at these wonderful clubs with their fifty thousand members and long waiting lists and described them to me as 'like a Woolies cafe in peak hour'.

I decided Sydney's nightlife was too much for me and headed home to watch TV. That was one of the really nice things about being in Sydney—knowing that, while we in Queensland merely produce wool, meat, sugar, and minerals for export to earn more money for the country, Sydney produces our TV programmes and advertising for us. And while we might come up with some champion Brahman bulls and disease-resistant cane varieties, they certainly know what sort of television to produce. There are all those intellectual shows like *Casino 10* (I changed channels in case it was illegal) and *Wheel of Fortune* and *Celebrity Game* where everyone squeals and laughs and spins wheels—so good are they in fact that I understand TV stations in America have copied the programmes exactly. And they blend in so well with the ads that we callow people in Queensland have difficulty telling when the show ends and the ads begin.

Saturday morning I slipped down to Double Bay. I had seen the giant homes that line the hillsides along Vaucluse and Rose Bay and although I couldn't go inside them at least I could see where the people shopped. It was great to see so many people doing well—what, with all the talk of recession and inflation and unemployment I was surprised to see people living in massive harbour-view homes driving down in their Rolls-Royces, E-type Jaguars and Porsches to do their shopping. The panache of the straw hat, the Pierre Balmain scarf, the cravat, the Gucci handbag pervaded the atmosphere.

One shop wrapped all Christmas presents in gold wrapping, another offered a 'valet service' instead of the more prosaic 'dry cleaning'. It was pleasing to see the imitation of the French with ladies' *coiffure* and *objets d'art*—and Medipet was available for one's pampered poodle. In two places even the takeaway food was in French—*galatine de poularde* or *mousee au grand*, and shops offered such exotic delicacies as rhubarb chutney.

Unfortunately it seems a lot of Sydney people can't live near that delightfully beautiful harbour. The cynics say that unless the house is a 'company' house few can afford the harbourside setting and I have heard Queenslanders refer to these as 'the gilded one per cent'. From what I could see, for the other 99 per cent of Sydneysiders the harbour, the bridge and the Opera House must look great on postcards to send away to friends.

In fact it was fun to get in a taxi and go out into the western suburbs to see where most Sydney people live. That Parramatta Road sure is one of the wonders of the world, emphasizing the vibrant lifestyle of a big metropolis—elongated queues of noisy cars, the smell of diesoline, the thousands and thousands of billboards lining the road, and a huge variety of used car yards to choose from. These western suburbs are very impressive. Every family has its own small red brick home with a red tile roof, and I liked the uniformity of design which Sydney has somehow managed to keep up for kilometre after kilometre. Out here the workers are lucky in that they almost never have to bother getting mixed up with the rich and the tourists around Sydney Harbour and the Opera House because Parramatta Road keeps them away.

The Opera House and the bridge were knockouts but I thought it wise not to hang around. Someone at Parliament House had twigged that I was a northerner and asked me how things were 'behind the Banana Curtain'.

I lowered myself further down in the taxi—a corrupt redneck from Queensland. I knew I was. I had been drinking and gambling at an illegal casino, viewing pornographic magazines and films in Kings Cross and generally enjoying myself.

I breathed more than a sigh of relief as the Boeing 727 took off and climbed out of the smog cloud under which Sydney lives. For the first time I understood the advertisement Qantas uses for its overseas flights in Brisbane: 'Why get landed with Sydney on your way to London?'

But I couldn't help wondering where that honest cop got to.

COPYRIGHT

First published in 1980 by University of Queensland Press

This edition published in 2021 by Ligature Pty Limited
34 Campbell St · Balmain NSW 2041 · Australia
www.ligatu.re · mail@ligatu.re

e-book ISBN: 9781922730459

ligature untapped

This print edition published in collaboration with Brio Books, an imprint of Booktopia Group Ltd

Level 6, 1A Homebush Bay Drive · Rhodes NSW 2138 · Australia

Print ISBN: 9781761281310

briobooks.com.au